Beyond the
Balanced Scorecard

Beyond the Balanced Scorecard

Improving Business Intelligence
With Analytics

Mark Graham Brown

New York

Most Productivity Press books are available at quantity discounts
when purchased in bulk. For more information contact our Customer
Service Department (888-319-5852). Address all other inquiries to:

Productivity Press
444 Park Avenue South, 7th Floor
New York, NY 10016
United States of America
Telephone: 212-686-5900
Fax: 212-686-5411
E-mail: info@productivitypress.com
ProductivityPress.com

Library of Congress Cataloging-in-Publication Data

Brown, Mark Graham.
    Beyond the balanced scorecard : improving business intelligence
with analytics / Mark Graham Brown.
        p. cm.
    Includes bibliographical references and index.
    ISBN 978-1-56327-346-9 (alk. paper)
    1. Organizational effectiveness—Evaluation.   2. Performance—
Management.   3. Business intelligence.   4. Business
mathematics.   I. Title.
HD58.9.B754   2007
658.4'013—dc22
                                                    2006035405

10   09   08   07   06   5   4   3   2   1

To Holli Orick Brown, whose laughter and love
I cherish more than anything.
—MGB

Contents

Foreword

A variety of performance management philosophies are well-defined and documented, but it is very difficult for organizations to apply these paradigms in concert with an existing business dynamic. Choosing a framework or model that is appropriate in a given culture, monitoring performance on an ongoing basis, and making business decisions based on facts and data are the underlying fundamentals of performance management. Yet many organizations embark on a performance management journey only to give up before achieving tangible results – it is too hard to follow all of the perceived rules!

The scenario is similar in spirit to the challenges faced by an orchestra; each individual instrument contributes uniquely, but if each instrument is not tuned and synchronized with the others, and not all individual players are focused on delivery of common music, the performance is a failure. Similarly, in a performance management journey the issue becomes one of having the right conductor to set a unified vision for the merging of paradigms to a common organizational philosophy. Mark offers a practical approach to help create and guide the performance management conductors.

Visionary organizations have proven that an engrained performance management culture is a necessary and fundamental business process that enables success over peers/competitors in all economic markets and conditions. For those new to performance management, there necessarily comes a realization that there is no right way to develop a performance management culture; there is no magic set of measures, and no management theory that will enable performance optimization in a vacuum of the human element. Instead, creatively adapting and applying key fundamentals of performance management theory and leveraging the human assets in the organization who understand the goals and the culture will produce the tangible results desired.

Typically, performance management initiatives are perceived from one of two polarized positions: some people foresee an easy solution to determine their scorecard measures, whereas others anticipate a complex solution. Moreover, there is often a large disconnect between what leaders need to know about their organization, what they want to know, and what they are measuring in their organization. True performance management success is achieved only when there is a balancing of these extremes, and by applying both art and science to define a suitable model.

Mark's approach helps to bridge the information gap by looking at organizations from a holistic perspective and illustrating drivers of performance management success. The approach to performance management is a practical one, which has been validated by real-life scenarios (both successes and failures). The philosophies can be applied at an individual level, a departmental level, or enterprise-wide, as well as across both the public and private sectors.

With the use of real world examples that span all performance management methodologies and industries, readers will be able to relate to, question, and challenge the proposed solutions, as well as extrapolate on the lessons to assist in their own specific circumstances. This book is full of insightful tools and best practices that will both support and enable a successful performance management journey, regardless of where you are on the performance management continuum.

Donna Jung

Acknowledgements

First of all, I would like to thank all of the clients over the last few years who have given me the opportunity to learn many of the lessons documented in this book. There are too many to list by name, but some are mentioned in the book and cited as examples of organizations with exceptional and innovative approaches and metrics.

I would also like to thank some individuals who took the time to give me valuable suggestions on the manuscript:

Dr. Gerald Blanton	AMSEC
Don Hoeffert	Storaenso
Stephanie W. Honda	University of Southern California
John M. Mullins	U.S. Department of the Interior
Michael J. Novak	U.S. Internal Revenue Service
Noriko Oyama, Daniel Kube, and Donna Jung	Performancesoft

Finally, I would like to thank Ruth Mills, who did a fantastic job editing the book and making it easier to read and follow, and Michael Sinocchi and the rest of the management of Productivity Press, which has been publishing my books since 1990.

Introduction

We all want to trust statistics. We feel better about the validity of information and data if it is chopped up into increments and numbers and presented on charts and graphs. Numbers and statistics are certainly more objective than gut-feel data. At the same time, we are aware that "trusted statistics" are not always as valid as they might be. We have become suspicious of survey data, knowing that it is fairly easy to manipulate this type of information. We have even come to suspect financial information, one type of data that people trusted the most because it measured real money and because there were strict accounting rules about how to count money in an organization. In the last 10 years, however, ethics problems in big corporations have taught us that financial results can also be falsified. A consequence of this is that many people no longer trust the stock market and many more don't trust big corporations and the numbers they report. Nevertheless, we still need a way of keeping score. We need a way to evaluate and quantify the performance of an organization.

Most consultants have one good book in them. If that book is even a moderate success, they keep rewriting it; the same book appears over and over with a slightly different twist on the same content. This is my third book on performance metrics and, yes, there is some review of some information from my previous books. However, since I wrote my first metrics book (*Keeping Score*) in 1996, I have learned a lot. I have also made a lot of mistakes and have tried some new things, some of which have worked quite well. The biggest lesson I have learned is that *deciding how to measure success is as important as figuring out the strategies for achieving success*. Another important lesson learned is that despite all the current attention accorded to metrics and balanced scorecards today, performance measurement in business, government, military, health care, or educational organizations is not very productive or successful. While performance measures are somewhat more sophisticated than in the past, most still lack integrity and do not tell leaders of these organizations what they want or need to know about some dimension of performance.

This book is about a new way to measure performance and health in an organization: the balanced scorecard. Introduced by Kaplan and Norton as a revolutionary approach to measurement in 1992, the balanced scorecard has led many organizations to add a broader array of metrics to their dashboards beyond the traditional financial and operational metrics. Since 1992, we have learned that the initial four categories of singular metrics (financial, customer, internal, and learning, innovation, and growth) that were the basis of the scorecard are not enough. We have also learned that we cannot measure the health of an enterprise by looking at a dozen statistics. Instead, what is needed is a new and more evolved scorecard with metrics that more accurately measure complicated dimensions of an organization's performance. If it were not for the work of Kaplan and Norton and their continuous refinement of the scorecard and how it can be used, this evolution would not have happened.

How This Book Is Organized

Chapter 1 provides some background on scorecards and metrics and describes best practices for creating your own. Chapters 2 and 3 go on to explain what the new scorecard ought to contain and what the new type of metrics, which I call *analytics*, look like. Chapters 4 through 8 describe recommended analytics that provide managers with answers to important questions about performance in their organizations in five key areas: customers, the external environment, people (i.e., your employees), operations, and strategy and financials. Each of these chapters ends with "key points to keep in mind" when determining the metrics you will use in your own organization. Feel free to copy and use all of the shaded figures in the book when you are working to improve your own metrics and performance.

Finally, Chapter 9 discusses recent developments in performance management that make the scorecard more than just a reporting tool. Links to knowledge databases, projects, external resources, and other data will be discussed. Linked to other data, the scorecard becomes both a better analytic tool and an aid to improving performance. In other words, the scorecard does not merely tell you if you are not performing to standard: It helps you decide *how to improve* performance.

The appendix to the book includes examples of scorecards that include analytics from a wide variety of organizations. These examples are presented to give you ideas for metrics you might want to include on your own scorecard. The examples are also a good way to see if you are tracking some of the same metrics being tracked by others in your industry or field.

How This Book Can Help You and Your Organization

What you will learn from this book is how to measure the things that are missing from most scorecards. Major aspects of organizational health are currently not being addressed in most scorecards. At best, anecdotal data is the only type of data that exists to evaluate the success of many important and expensive business strategies. This book provides guidance on how to quantify and regularly track progress on a wide variety of factors that are difficult to measure. In addition, dozens of figures provide examples—both from business and non-profit and government organizations—and the shaded figures are intended for use as guidelines when developing your own metrics and analytics. You will learn how to answer the following questions about what you measure in your organization:

- Are we building positive relationships with the right customers to grow the business and build their loyalty?
- Are we going after the right types of new business?
- Are we doing what it takes to make customers happy and not irritate them?
- What is our brand image?
- What is going on in the world that might impact our organization's success?
- What sort of competitive threats should we be watching?
- What type of relationships do we have with our important partners and suppliers?

- How are we doing at meeting regulatory requirements?
- How satisfied and engaged are our employees?
- How healthy and safe are our employees?
- How are we doing on diversity and ethics?
- Do we have the right people with the right knowledge and skills?
- Are we effectively communicating to our people?
- How are we doing on our major projects?
- Are we managing our key processes effectively?
- Are we making the most productive use of our resources?
- Are we effectively minimizing risks?
- Is our organization financially healthy?
- How are we doing at new product/service development?
- How are we doing on the key strategies linked to our vision?
- How are we doing on major performance improvement initiatives?

The best performance measures are not single variables. The best performance measures are made up of a grouping of individual statistics that provide a more objective and well-rounded view of a dimension of performance. Read on and learn how to create a *new* type of scorecard that tells you what you *really* need to know about how your organization is performing.

Beyond the
Balanced Scorecard

1

Beyond First-Generation Balanced Scorecards

Performance measurement in organizations is not something new, but in the last 30 years or so, organizations have realized that financial measures alone are not sufficient for evaluating the success of an enterprise. In the 1970s, productivity became a big concern, and business and government organizations began tracking the productivity of labor, machinery, and other resources. In the 1980s, we all became concerned with quality and customer satisfaction, so those measures became part of organizational scorecards.

In the mid-1990s, the balanced scorecard concept was introduced, forcing executives to take a hard look at how many of their metrics were financial and then balance out their scorecards with nonfinancial metrics. The balanced scorecard approach also recommended that fewer are better: The number of metrics that companies tracked had been increasing each year for many years, but Kaplan and Norton suggested that no one should have more than 15 to 20 metrics per scorecard. This is still a tough sell for analytical executives who love poring over hundreds of charts each month.

Evolution of the Balanced Scorecard

Over the last 30 years or so, the approaches that organizations use to measure performance have gone through three clear phases or stages. Each phase has lasted 10 or 15 years, and with each successive phase, the practice of measuring performance has become more exact. The process is still a long way from what you would call science, but the measures are improving, as is the integrity of the data. Models like the Baldrige criteria have helped facilitate this systematic approach to measuring and managing performance. Figure 1-1 shows the evolution of the balanced scorecard.

Evolution of Scorecards

1995–2005
• Balanced scorecard adopted
• 12–20 metrics typical
• Customer, financial, internal and
  growth metrics
• All singular metrics
• Customer & employee metrics
  annual and based on surveys
• Spreadsheets and
  PowerPoints used
  to review data

2006
• Most metrics analytics
• Application to education and
  healthcare and government
• Scorecards deployed to multiple
  levels
• Use of scorecard software
• Definition of links between metrics
• Scorecards for all employees

Early 1990's
More measures are better
• Many quality metrics
• 30 to 50 metrics common
• All singular metrics
• Metrics for many levels — not just executives

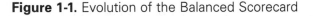
• Mostly financial and operational metrics
• All lagging indicators
• Productivity metrics
• All singular metrics

Figure 1-1. Evolution of the Balanced Scorecard

Stage I Scorecards: Focusing on Financial and Operational Metrics

Prior to 1980 or so, organizations measured their performance by reviewing a wide variety of operational and financial statistics and ratios: Figure 1-2 shows a typical scorecard from this time period. Executives sat in monthly meetings and often looked at more than 30 metrics, which were all lagging measures and almost all financial. A few forward-thinking companies tracked things like customer satisfaction or employee morale once a year, and many had productivity measures on their scorecards. In fact, productivity was the big buzz-word of the 1970s, so many different productivity ratios were often examined: labor productivity, capital productivity, equipment productivity, etc. In some case, executives thought it might also be important to measure product defects or how long it takes before a product fails in the field (MTBF, or mean time between failures).

All of the measures in a Stage 1 scorecard are important, but there are too many of them, they are all lagging, and they are not balanced. A number of companies today still use Stage 1 scorecards. In fact, a recent review of scorecards of several major corporations shows that they include more than 30 metrics, and about 90 percent of the measures are either financial or operational. If your scorecard looks like the example in Figure 1-2, you are probably not ready for analytics as metrics. Instead, you need to focus on basics, such as reducing the number of metrics on your scorecard and adding in measures that assess dimensions like customer and employee satisfaction.

Typical Stage 1 Scorecard					
Financial Metrics					
Sales Revenue	Gross Margin	Accounts Receivable	Assets/ Liabilities	EBITDA	Stock Price
Budget	Costs	Headcount	R&D $	Profit	Growth
Operational Metrics					
Production Units	Defects	On-Time Delivery	Labor Productivity	Equipment Productivity	Raw Matl. Productivity
# of New Products	Training Hours	Patents	MTBF	Accidents	Audit Scores

Figure 1-2. Stage 1 Scorecard

Stage II Scorecards: Adding Quality Metrics

Beginning in about 1980, organizations started to become obsessed with quality and customer satisfaction. Experts in the field, particularly Phil Crosby and W. Edwards Deming, were in big demand and taught companies how to reduce defects and improve customer satisfaction.

Process analysis and improvement also became quite popular. Michael Hammer and his colleagues made a lot of money teaching companies an approach to process improvement, which he called "reengineering." Companies formed teams and starting mapping their processes and looking for ways to improve efficiency and quality. Scorecards went from 30 or more measures to more than 50. The same old financial and operational metrics still needed to be reviewed, but were now compounded by new measures of quality, customer satisfaction, and process improvement.

During this phase, the prevailing logic was that the more measures you had, the more intelligently you could run your organization. Armies of people were employed to prepare charts and graphs for monthly meetings so that the organization could look at more data. Of course, many Stage II scorecards are still out there, along with their Stage I counterparts. Figure 1-3 shows a typical scorecard from this time period.

Typical Stage 2 Scorecard

Financial Metrics

Sales Revenue	Gross Margin	Accounts Receivable	Assets/ Liabilities	EVA	Stock Price
Budget	Costs	Headcount	R&D $	Profit	Growth

Operational Metrics

Production Units	Labor Productivity	Equipment Productivity	Raw Matl. Productivity	# of New Products	Training Hours
Accidents	MTBF	Patents	Audit Scores	On-Time Delivery	

Quality Metrics

Cost of Poor Quality	Defects	Rework	Suggestions Per Employee	Quality Audit Scores
Processes	Processes	# of Teams	Baldrige/ISO	Awards
Customer Surveys	Warranty Claims	Complaints	Benchmarking Studies	Competitive Rankings
Turnover	Training Plans Completed		Training$/Payroll	

Figure 1-3. Typical Stage II Scorecards 1980–1995

Stage III Scorecards: Including Measures from More Stakeholders

Between 1992 and 1996, the concept of the balanced scorecard, a term first coined by Robert Kaplan and David Norton, really began taking off, and new books on performance metrics (including my own *Keeping Score*, 1996) were published. Companies were coming to the realization that fewer measures are better and that they needed to balance out their metrics to look at how they were performing for various stakeholder groups, such as customers and shareholders. This approach was also taking hold in healthcare, education, and government organizations. The federal government passed an act called the Government Performance and Results Act (GPRA), which basically said that government organizations need to have performance metrics that focus on outcomes they are creating for taxpayers and others. In connection with this, most government organizations adopted some version of the balanced scorecard approach.

Over the last 10 years, scorecards in most organizations have become more manageable. Focusing on fewer metrics, they have become more balanced, and they now include measures of customers, employees, and other stakeholders. Even the Baldrige criteria, which is the most widely accepted model for organizational excellence, calls for a balanced scorecard approach to metrics (although the model does not specifically used the phrase "balanced scorecard").

A typical balanced scorecard today still includes mostly lagging metrics, and every measure is a single statistic designed to measure a complex dimension of performance. For example, employee morale is assessed using a single annual survey, or safety is evaluated by counting accidents. Figure 1-4 shows what a typical scorecard today might look like.

APQC's Findings Regarding Measurement Best Practices

In 2004, I had the privilege of working with the American Productivity and Quality Center (APQC) in Houston on an important study that was designed to identify what major corporations are doing in the way of performance measurement. This comprehensive study began

Typical Stage III Scorecard				
Financial Metrics				
Sales	Profits/EBITDA	Growth	Costs Stock	ROI
Customer Metrics				
Customer Survey	Customer Complaints		Market Share	Loyalty
Internal Metrics				
Production	Cycle Time	Quality	Safety	Productivity
Learning, Innovation & Growth				
Employee Survey	Training Hours	Turnover	$ of New Products	Suggestions Per Employee

Figure 1-4. Typical Stage III Scorecards 1996–2005

with about 80 companies that completed detailed questionnaires about their scorecards and use of performance metrics.

One encouraging finding of the study was that only 24 percent of the 80 companies surveyed tracked only traditional accounting and operational measures. This means that more than three-fourths of the companies in the study had scorecards that were more balanced than previously used scorecards. Of the 76 percent that had nontraditional metrics, 28 percent described their collection of metrics as a "balanced scorecard," although this 28 percent should probably be considered a low figure, because many organizations think their scorecards are not balanced if they do not strictly follow Kaplan and Norton's four suggested categories of metrics: financial, customer, internal, and learning, innovation, and growth.

Beginning with this initial list of 80 companies, APQC narrowed down its study to a small number of companies that would serve as good benchmarks for others with regard to performance measurement. Five companies that had different and interesting approaches to performance measurement were highlighted in the APQC study: Bank of America, Saturn, L.L. Bean, Crown Castle, and Jet Blue. It is interesting to note that the companies selected range from huge (Bank of America) to small (Crown Castle) and from old (L.L. Bean) to young (Jet Blue). Although all five of these companies had good balanced scorecards, none were without areas needing further refine-ment. In other words, even some of the best companies in the world are struggling to come up with just the right metrics to drive employee behavior and decision making. Thus, if your organization is also strug-gling with this challenge, you are in good company.

Results of the APQC Study of Measurement Best Practices

One of the positive findings of this study was that the better companies had scorecards that met the following guidelines:

- **Scorecards should be tailored to the age and complexity of the business.** Jet Blue's scorecard is fine for a company just getting started, whereas Bank of America's metrics are more complex and evolved because the company has been in the banking business for many years.
- **Scorecards should be linked to goals and strategies.** The better companies in the study showed clear links between vision, goals, and strategy and what was measured on their scorecards.
- **Scorecards should be balanced across their stakeholders.** The scorecards included 3 to 5 customer, financial, operational, customer, people, and other categories of metrics.
- **Scorecards should be deployed to levels beyond senior management.** Several of the companies selected by APQC as benchmarks had deployed the scorecard approach to several layers of management.

Of the 80 or so companies examined by APQC, scorecards varied from Stage I to Stage III. The five companies that were selected as the benchmarks or best all had Stage III scorecards that were fairly close to the example shown in Figure 1-4.

Performance Management in Europe

Adopting a more balanced approach to performance measurement is not strictly an American phenomenon. A paper by Veronica Martinez from the Cranfield School of Management in the United Kingdom suggests that 57 percent of UK companies and 26 percent of German and Austrian companies have adopted the balanced scorecard approach. Although many European companies have adopted this approach, however, Dr. Martinez's research reveals as many negatives as positives. Managers in companies that had implemented new scorecards noted that using them was time consuming, costly, complicated, misleading, and mechanistic. However, none of these problems can be attributed to a more balanced approach for measuring performance, and all are certainly avoidable.

The negatives attributed to performance measurement are the same flaws that can be associated with just about any strategy for improving performance: The process is difficult and complicated, people cheat, and it is not a guarantee of good performance. The same things can be said of diet and exercise, which clearly increase the probability of a healthy long life. We all know of people who have died despite a healthy lifestyle, but no one questions the benefits of healthy living, even if this is sometimes difficult to achieve. If we extend this analogy, performance measurement is difficult to do well, but the payoffs can be enormous.

Problems with Most Scorecards Today: The New Top 10 List

Although most organizations have come a long way (it has taken almost 40 years) in introducing better metrics on their corporate scorecards, there is still much work to be done, and even the best scorecards need improvement in some areas. My second book on developing scorecards (*Winning Score*, 2000) included my top 10 list of stupid measurement practices. My observations over the last six years suggest it is time for a new list. Since 2000, organizations have had ample experience and ample time to refine their scorecards, so you'd expect that they would have improved quite a bit. Sadly, that is not the case. Some of my findings from reviewing the current scorecards of government and business organizations are summarized in Figure 1-5 and described in the following sections.

Problem #1: Most Metrics Are Lagging

The vast majority of measures on scorecards are still measures of the past. For example:

1. Most metrics are lagging.
2. No one is measuring ethics.
3. Problems still exist in aligning goals, strategies, and metrics.
4. Scorecards are not deployed beyond senior management levels.
5. Most executive bonuses are not linked to nonfinancial metrics.
6. Most targets are still set arbitrarily.
7. Customer satisfaction metrics are still rudimentary and lack refinement.
8. Human resource metrics are still close to worthless.
9. PowerPoint and spreadsheets are still being used to review performance.
10. Scorecards never include external factors that could have a huge impact on an organization's success.

Figure 1-5. The Top 10 Problems With Most Scorecards Today

- Almost all financial measures are lagging indicators.
- Measures of employee morale and safety are often limited to turnover and lost-time accidents.
- Operational measures like productivity, defects, and milestones met on projects are also measures of the past.

A good balance is to have no more than a third of the metrics on your scorecard be lagging, but my observations reveal that close to 75 percent of metrics on scorecards today are measures of the past. Although lagging metrics of outcomes like sales, profits, and loyal customers are important, they are the least manageable measures of all because performance has already passed.

Problem #2: No One Is Measuring Ethics

In the last five years, we have seen many large organizations go into Chapter 11 bankruptcy or even worse. By the time your CEO is being led away in handcuffs, you don't need to look at the scorecard to tell you there is an ethics problem in the company. But even with all the attention currently directed at the importance of ethics, I have not encountered a single major corporation or government organization that has an ethics metric on its scorecard.

Problem #3: Problems Still Exist in Aligning Goals, Strategies, and Metrics

Too many organizations still have goals and strategies for which there are no metrics on the scorecards. For example, one organization had a goal to improve communication, yet it had no means of measuring whether communication had improved. Another had a goal of becoming a great place to work for employees, but it had no way to measure that on the scorecard, other than turnover. Moreover, millions of dollars are being spent on new software, management programs, and other initiatives without any clear tie to one of the scorecard metrics that should show improvement.

Problem #4: Scorecards Are Not Deployed Beyond Senior Management Levels

The majority of work that gets done in an organization is done by workers and supervisors, not senior leaders. Yet many organizations with excellent scorecards have failed to develop scorecards for departments, supervisors, and individual contributors. All levels of employees need to have a scorecard that tells them how they are performing on their job responsibilities. Sharing managers' scorecards with employees is not the same as having your own scorecard.

Problem #5: Most Executive Bonuses Are Not Linked to Nonfinancial Metrics

A number of big corporations I have worked with have good balance in their scorecards, but executive compensation is still linked to a handful of lagging financial measures, such as growth and profit. Often, this causes leaders to ignore nonfinancial metrics. There are some forward-thinking companies like FedEx that are confident enough in their customer and people metrics to link them to bonuses, but such companies are in the minority.

Problem #6: Most Targets Are Still Set Arbitrarily

Establishing red, yellow, and green targets or ranges is as important as the metric itself. Unfortunately, many targets are still set without reference to competitor performance, industry averages, or benchmarks. Establishing a target that is too high or too low will not drive the right decision making and actions. I still see a lot of arbitrary stretch targets, with no thought given to the resources needed to achieve those targets or how achievement of one target may cause a decline in performance on another company metric.

Problem #7: Customer Satisfaction Metrics Are Still Rudimentary and Lack Refinement

Measures of customer satisfaction and relationships should be directly linked to growth and profits, but many organizations are still relying on crude surveys that are done too infrequently to be of much use. Complaints are the other common customer satisfaction metric, but this data is not a good indicator because most unhappy customers do not complain—they leave. Asking whether or not a customer would recommend your firm is the latest fad in this area (a topic discussed in more detail below), but this question elicits very little useful data.

Problem #8: Human Resource Metrics Are Still Close to Worthless

People measures on the scorecards of most organizations are usually turnover, training hours, and an annual survey. Most of these measures are of dubious value. Attempts to measure corporate culture, knowledge management, and intellectual capital are admirable, but the metrics are rarely accurate or useful. In spite of how bad the metrics are in this area, companies have no problem spending millions on knowledge management systems, leadership training, corporate culture programs, and team building, with only anecdotal data to measure their effectiveness.

Problem #9: PowerPoints and Spreadsheets Are Still Being Used to Review Performance

Most organizations still use PowerPoint presentations and prepare reports of performance using spreadsheets that are difficult to read and interpret. The dreaded monthly review meeting has not changed much, even in organizations that have adopted more balanced scorecards. Excellent scorecard software exists that is not being used even by organizations that own it. There is some very poorly designed scorecard software on the market as well. One such business intelligence

(BI) software program is so complicated to use that even scientists at one of our top national laboratories don't use it.

Problem #10: Scorecards Never Include External Factors That Could Have a Huge Impact on an Organization's Success

One of the big factors a pilot needs to monitor is weather. Although the pilot cannot do anything about the weather, not having weather gauges in the cockpit would be unthinkable, a risk to safety and a huge mistake. The equivalent to weather gauges on an organization's scorecard might include factors such as the economy, the price of raw materials used by the firm, political trends, strategies of specific competitors, regulatory factors, brand image, and a number of other variables. A good balanced scorecard should include these external factors that are just as important as the company's own performance. Even though you can't control these factors any better than a pilot can control the weather, knowing they exist and what they imply for your organization can help you avoid turbulence. In spite of this, it is difficult to find a corporate or government scorecard that includes a weather gauge. Consequently, leaders are often making decisions and developing action plans based on how well the plane is operating, rather than on the conditions in which it is operating as well.

Although there are more dubious scorecard metrics and approaches than good ones, there are some best practices that deserve mention here. Some of the best practices simply do the opposite of the 10 dumb things listed above. Other best practices are described in the following sections.

Best Practice #1: Kill Flawed Metrics

This is probably the most prevalent problem with scorecards. Organizations put old metrics on their new scorecards even though everyone knows that performance on the measures can be easily manipulated. I have seen this happen in several different military organizations that wanted to have a measure of project schedule performance on their new balanced scorecards that I was helping them design. The concept behind the metric was solid: It measured percent milestones completed on major projects. Past performance on this measure showed it was always green throughout the course of a given project, yet customers' biggest complaint was that the organizations failed to meet major project deadlines.

The problem with this measure was that the scheduled dates were always changed or adjusted when project managers saw that they were going to be missed. It was easy to justify the new deadlines because of changes to project scope or delays from suppliers/ vendors. Throughout the course of a project, the schedule gauge looked green until the very end, when it turned red because the end date was missed. The main problem with this measure was that the schedule data lacked integrity—it was too easy for project managers to adjust the milestone dates to give the appearance that they were on schedule.

An organization that builds and maintains ships for the U.S. Navy came up with a better approach. It measured the amount of "churn" or change there is to a project's scope, schedule, and budget. Some amount of churn is expected and acceptable, but too much indicated either a poor project plan, or a poorly managed project. Churn was easy to track because the data came right from the project management software that everyone used to monitor project progress.

When people are allowed to select their own performance metrics, there is a tendency for them to pick measures that make them look good or can be easily manipulated. An objective outside facilitator such as a consultant can help minimize this self-serving approach, but it is often easy to snow the consultant or convince him or her that the proposed measures are valid. By the same token, internal facilitators often get overruled by senior managers. What ends up happening is that the new scorecard is no better than the old one. People go to meetings each month and look at the red, yellow, and green charts, but everyone knows that actual performance is often much different from what is depicted in the reports.

A solution to this common phenomenon is to use a separate group of inside or outside experts to review proposed metrics to look for data integrity problems. You might take your draft scorecard to several outside experts and ask them to spend a day or so reviewing the metrics and provide feedback. It is also a good idea to have some of your own people do this. Incorporating reviews like this can go a long way toward weeding out the bad metrics.

Best Practice #2: Measure Frequently

There is no business in the world that would think of measuring financial performance once a year. Instead, most managers and entrepreneurs measure financial and operational performance *daily*. The more often you measure something, the better you can manage it. For example, diabetics monitor their blood sugar several times a day; some people monitor their blood pressure every day. Fortunately, most business and government organizations seem to agree with this concept and have no problem with the cost and time it takes to monitor financial and operational performance on a daily and weekly basis.

On the other hand, if you look at these same organizations and ask them how often they measure customer satisfaction, employee satisfaction, and other "softer," but no less important aspects of their performance, they usually say, "Once a year." In fact, one company I work with measures employee satisfaction every *other* year. The score went down last year, so company executives are busily working on many initiatives to improve morale. When asked how things were going, they replied, "We don't know, we need to wait another 20 months to get another data point." With such a lengthy time frame, this organization may end up wasting a lot of money and time working on initiatives that do absolutely nothing to improve employee satisfaction.

The take-home message here is that if something is important enough to measure at all, you need to measure it *frequently*. Annual metrics are close to worthless, and they function more like a historical study rather than as a performance measure. Of course, the more frequently you measure something, the more it usually costs. The challenge is to come up with a way to measure performance often without spending a lot of money. This is both practical and feasible.

One client, for example, used to spend $100,000 a year to have some university conduct an annual survey of employee satisfaction. A team came up with the idea of measuring morale on a daily basis by giving all employees a bag of red, yellow, and green marbles. At the end of the day, employees now drop a marble in a vase by the door where they usually leave, depending on how good or bad of a day they had (red = a really bad day, yellow = a fair day, and green = a really good day). Each morning, the boss's assistant counts up the marbles by department, and managers talk to their people if there are a lot of red or yellow marbles from the previous day. The entire system costs less than $1,000 a year to implement, provides a daily statistic on morale by department, and forces managers to talk to their people on a daily basis about working conditions and other issues.

Another client used to spend more than $100,000 each year for an annual customer survey that was used to produce a big report and a once-a-year data point. This company also discovered that customer satisfaction data did not correlate to customer loyalty. To correct the discrepancy, it came up with a "Customer Aggravation Index" that it could track on a daily basis. The index measured operational and quality problems that were already being tracked, things that tend to make customers angry, such as being put on hold when calling the call center, late deliveries, errors on invoices, etc. The company found a direct correlation between levels of customer aggravation and loyalty. In other words, the measure confirmed that screwing up and making customers angry resulted in customers taking their business elsewhere—usually without bothering to fill out a stupid survey. This metric costs very little to implement, because most of the aggravations were already being tracked.

Best Practice #3: Keep It Simple

I can't tell you how many organizations I have worked with that have designed scorecards with perfect symmetry, logical architecture, and a balance of measures that look at the past, present, and future. The designs of these scorecards are vastly superior to those of any of the five companies identified by APQC as having benchmarkable scorecards. Yet, most of these organizations have failed to *build* most of the cool metrics they designed, and many of the gauges on their new dashboard remain gray—in other words, there is no data.

Overcomplicating the scorecard seems to be more common in technical organizations that have lots of engineers, but this is not always the case. For example, several government social-service-type organizations have managed to do the same thing without involving any engineers in the scorecard design process. It is encouraging that organizations want to measure all sorts of important things like ethics, customer relationships, and intellectual capital, but most of these softer things end up being very hard to measure. It is much more rational for an organization to design a scorecard with 12 gauges that will actually be filled with data in the next year than to design a framework with 22 metrics while collecting data on only 6 of them.

Two approaches work well when designing the scorecard architecture. First, design it using metrics you know you can populate with data in the next 6 to 12 months, realizing that you can always add new measures later, as you become more adept at metric design and implementation. It may be tough to get people to agree to this, but keep reminding them that the scorecard should evolve and change with time, so no one is expected to get it exactly right the first time.

A second approach, which works even better, is to design the ideal scorecard with all the measures leaders want and need to look at, but build it gradually over several years. The Santa Clara Valley Water District has adopted this approach. Its CEO scorecard includes about 20 metrics, but it is going to take at least three years to populate each of them with data. The district has developed a plan that shows a progression from initially "lighting up" about 10 of the measures with data and then working up to all of them over three years. The chance of the scorecard changing over a three-year period is also quite high for most organizations. New problems and challenges arise, bosses change, new goals are set, and all of these things tend to drive a change in the performance measures of an organization.

Best Practice #4: Get on With It

Another common problem with scorecard projects is that they tend to experience analysis paralysis. In other words, everyone wants to review the scorecard design and add, delete, or somehow change the metrics. And most of the time, the proposals are very valid and worth considering. It is important to understand, however, that these reviews slow down the process considerably.

For example, a Navy organization went through about four drafts of the CO's scorecard over a period of a year. Each time a new group reviewed it, changes were made. In an effort to get buy-in from as many people as possible, leaders wanted to get lots of input. Although this sounds good in theory, it rarely works well. The scorecard project ends up being stalled in the design phase, and measures never get built or implemented because the architects keep redrawing the blueprints.

A better approach, one used by several recent clients, is to tell people up front that the scorecard is just a first draft and that it will be changed and improved each year as the organization gets more sophisticated. One organization that did this effectively is the City of Los Angeles Workforce Development Division, which assigned two of its best people to design its new scorecard, spent half a day reviewing it with senior management, and is getting on with the process of defining each of the metrics and developing data collection plans. People are comfortable with the approach, because they know that the measures and scorecard design will be improved each year. They recognize that mistakes will be made and are a normal part of the design process.

This approach of just getting on with the project is vastly superior to months and months of review and revision cycles in scorecard architecture and metrics design. You should change the metrics once you see that they are not useful and minimize changes during the design phase. A Navy client, Carrier Team One, which does maintenance on aircraft carriers, has adopted this approach, and it has made a lot of progress over the last few years in actually collecting data on most of the metrics it identified several years ago.

Stage IV Scorecards: Balanced Measurements for 2006 and Beyond

Figure 1-6 shows a typical balanced scorecard. There are a number of dimensions that characterize a Phase IV scorecard:

- There are more predictive metrics and fewer lagging ones.
- There are very few singular metrics on executives' scorecards.
- Metrics are better aligned with goals, strategies, and plans.
- All improvement initiatives are linked to one or more scorecard metrics.
- Scorecards are not just for leaders and managers; all levels of employees need scorecards.

- Scorecard data are presented electronically without PowerPoint charts and spreadsheets.
- Metrics on the scorecard are the real numbers used to run the business.
- High-level metrics are made of a number of layers of sub-metrics.
- Strategy maps and research are used to develop process and leading indicators.
- Performance review meetings involve looking at live real-time data, not prepared charts of history.

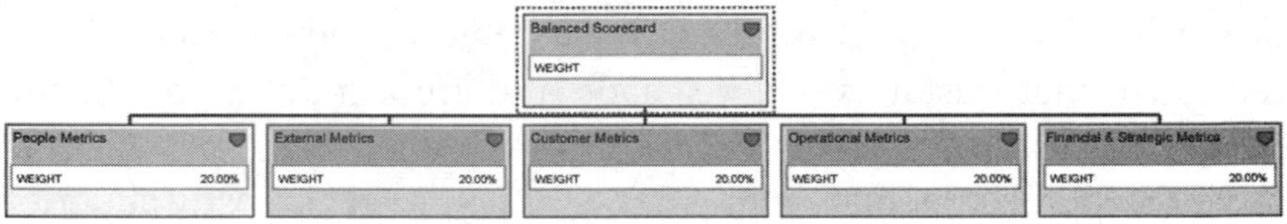

Figure 1-6. Typical Stage IV Scorecard

Summary & Conclusions

Performance measurement and management have clearly taken hold both in the United States and in Europe. Most forward-thinking business and government organizations have implemented a measurement structure that includes more than the traditional lagging measures of financial and operational performance. Nevertheless, many scorecard projects fail because of either poor design or poor implementation. In contrast, successful projects are characterized by an approach that:

- Eliminates old flawed metrics and replaces them with ones with good integrity;
- Includes metrics that can be tracked frequently (e.g., quarterly or monthly);
- Is a simple scorecard architecture that will actually be implemented; and
- Focuses on actual tracking of the new metrics rather than continually redrawing the scorecard to try to make it perfect.

Now that you have an idea of what a Stage IV scorecard looks like, you are ready to learn about how to construct a new type of metric called an *analytic*. Chapter 2 explains why this new metric is superior to singular statistics and how to construct various types of analytics to improve your business intelligence.

2

Analytics:
A New Way of Tracking
Organizational Performance

People love to look for that one magic number that will tell them every-thing they need to know. For example, many people are always concerned with their weight, and some people weigh themselves each day, obsessing when the scale reads a few pounds heavier than yesterday. Others obsess about their cholesterol or blood pressure, tracking it on a regular basis. Business people obsess about numbers. Most want to track sales figures on a daily basis and monitor costs at least weekly to make sure that their companies will be profitable. However, assessing the health of a business or person is not as simple as looking at a few good statistics.

This chapter reviews the types of performance data typically tracked by most organizations, reviews some of the "fad" metrics of recent years, and then defines and describes **analytics** in detail and the benefits of using them.

Types of Performance Data

Measuring performance of any kind of job—whether performed by a worker or a CEO—requires four types of performance data. These four types of data are described in the following sections.

Observational Performance Data

Another way to describe observational performance data is *walking around data*. You can learn a lot about how an organization performs by just being there and experiencing it. This type of data can be very revealing—especially if people don't know you are watching.

Starbucks and Jet Blue realize the importance of this type of data. Both companies require their executives to spend time on the front line every month. Starbucks executives work in actual stores, pouring coffee, taking orders, and sometimes even taking out the trash. This keeps them in touch with real customers, employees, and the operation. Jet Blue has a similar approach, except the company does not make its executives fly planes or load bags. Instead, Jet Blue executives make it a point to fly on the airline as regular passengers several times a month. Sam Walton, founder of Wal-Mart, subscribed to this management style as well; he could sometimes be found helping dock workers unload trucks or answering customers' questions in the store.

There is no substitute for spending time where the real work is done and keeping your eyes and ears open. This type of data is essential and should be regularly collected by all managers.

Progress Report Data

This type of data is a little more structured than just walking around and watching. To obtain this type of information, you actually have to ask people for information. We've all been to meetings where this is the only type of data reviewed. For example, the boss goes around the table and asks each salesperson what is going on with his or her existing accounts as well as his or her bids and prospects—in other words: "How's it going?"

This type of data is used to assess a wide variety of activities in an organization—far too many for my taste. People learn quickly to keep their reports positive and brief, so the boss does not start asking second- and third-level questions, such as "How's that Six Sigma program we've spent $6 million on working, Judy?" Such broad questions lead to broad answers that don't say enough about anything. Judy, for example, will respond, "Great, sir, we have made some real strides in getting a number of Black Belts trained, and we are evaluating and improving 13 of our major processes right now with some of our best people on the teams." But this answer is a progress report that deals in generalities and does not address anything specific about actual performance.

Progress report data does have its place, however. It is not reasonable or practical to try to turn everything into a graph with statistics. Sometimes a complete answer to the "How's it going?" question is just the type of data needed. For example, in small businesses, this is the vast majority of data used to run an enterprise. The boss is usually a worker as well, so he or she gets lots of observational data by doing real work all day long. What the boss doesn't know by being there and observing, he or she can ask. The only statistics small businesses tend to track are financial.

Study Results

This type of data results from studies, audits, assessments, or consulting projects designed to investigate some aspect of performance in an organization. For example, a study might be done to evaluate the potential market for a new variation of a product that you currently have in your portfolio. Another example might be an HR study on the effectiveness of your leadership development program, and outside consultants might be hired to evaluate the program and come back with quantitative and qualitative data on the program's effectiveness. Studies and research are important and provide quantifiable answers to important questions an organization may have.

Study results are not the same as the metrics that go on your scorecard, however, because they usually represent *a single data point*. For example, suppose you do a study and find out that the new software you installed doesn't produce the big ROI numbers the salespeople promised: This is a fact or a single data point, not an ongoing metric that belongs on the scorecard. The study has already provided you with the information you wanted to know. What differentiates study results from scorecard metrics is that studies are specific projects designed to find out something. The scorecard, on the other hand, *provides data on how well the organization does at its day-to-day work*.

Quantifiable Scorecard Performance Data

This fourth type of data consists of numbers, which are derived either from counting things (like money, complaints, or lost customers) or having someone make a judgment by rating or ranking performance on some scale (like surveys, focus groups, or scores). To gather this type of data, someone has to develop a data collection plan (and often an instrument) and collect and plot the data on some sort of graph or chart. For this type of quantifiable data to make sense, you need to establish targets or ranges defining what good performance looks like.

As organizations grow in size, they tend to collect more of this type of data and conduct more studies. In fact, many organizations employ small armies of accountants, statisticians, engineers, and others whose entire job is to measure and report various numbers. Even an organization that employs only one person needs some of this quantifiable performance data. For example, I measure a few financial statistics (such as revenue and accounts payable), but I also track repeat business from customers and attendance at my seminars, and I have found that book sales are a leading indicator for my consulting and training business. Even a small organization needs to keep track of some performance numbers, and they should not all be financial.

A scorecard, dashboard, or whatever analogy you prefer is nothing more than a collection of these quantifiable performance metrics. It is important to underscore, however, that the best scorecard in the world will not replace the other three types of data. If you spend all of your time sitting in meetings or your office looking at your scorecard charts, you are very likely to encounter some unpleasant surprises. In other words, you will lose touch with your operation. Improving the completeness and integrity of your performance measures will go a long way toward helping you make better decisions and develop good strategy, but it does not take the place of the other types of data. They are equally important.

Some Recent Fad Metrics

In recent years, new metrics have been invented that business people get enamored with for a while. They eventually get discouraged when the new metric does not tell them everything they need to know. For example, remember *cost of quality*? That was a popular new metric that appeared in the late 1980s. Phil Crosby made millions teaching organizations how to calculate the true cost of poor-quality products and services. Many organizations put this new metric on the scorecards of executives, who monitored it frequently. Many of these executives formed countless teams that worked on reducing the cost of poor quality. The concept behind this metric was solid, but the reason you no longer find this metric on the scorecards of organizations is that *it lacked integrity*: It was too easy for people to manipulate the numbers by doing things like not counting rework as rework. This metric died about 1995, but it has been reincarnated as Six Sigma cost savings. This new incarnation of cost of quality is basically the same metric with a little more integrity than the old cost of quality. With either the old or new metric, it is hard to find a bank account that has amassed all those promised savings.

Customer Satisfaction Surveys

This is another type of metric that became popular in the last 20 years. It started with the car companies and some hotels and restaurants, and now every type of organization from your dentist to your kids' school sends you a survey to measure your satisfaction.

This is another case of *a great idea, but poor execution*. Organizations found that customer satisfaction scores went up, but profits did not. In fact, some found an inverse relationship. As they spent more and more money to satisfy demanding customers, profits went down. Many did not even find a link between customer satisfaction and *loyalty*. Happy customers still take their business elsewhere when given a more attractive offer.

Customer satisfaction data is also easy to manipulate by surveying only happy customers, writing questions that force a favorable response, or offering customers incentives for high ratings on the survey. People in my workshops, for example, tell stories of car dealerships offering free services (e.g., detailing, oil changes, etc.) to customers in return for high ratings on customer satisfaction surveys.

Economic Value-Added (EVA) Metrics

This was such a popular metric for a few years that it made the cover of *Fortune* and other business magazines. It was supposed to be a more accurate way of looking at the financial performance of a company than traditional metrics like profit or EBITDA. EVA included the cost of capital and other factors that are not in traditional measures of profitability. The inventors of this new metric wrote an 800-page book about it called *The Quest for Value*. Yet, nowhere in the 800 pages do they tell you exactly *how to calculate* EVA. There was, in fact, so much technical mystery involved in calculating EVA that only the most experienced and expensive management consultants could be trusted to do the computations. Not surprisingly, many big corporations bought into this and wrote big checks to have the consultants compute their EVA performance. It turned out that this new metric fell out of favor over time when companies got tired of paying the consultants. The biggest problem with EVA was that no one understood it. Any metric that is so complicated that you need consultants to compute it is not likely to stay for long on the corporate dashboard. I have not seen or heard of any company tracking EVA in at least 5 years.

Willingness-to-Recommend Surveys

Rather than survey customers with a long series of questions, this new metric involves only one: **"What is your willingness to recommend this product or service to others on a 1–10 scale?"**

GE is so excited about this new metric that its chief quality officer is quoted in Business Week as saying, "This will be as big and long lasting as Six Sigma was."[1]

This new measure makes a lot more sense than adding up average ratings on 10 to 20 questions that vary in importance from a customer survey. Taking a bottom-line approach and asking customers whether they would recommend your firm makes a lot of sense. The logic is that customers who give you 9 or 10 ratings are big fans and are likely to promote your company to others. Detractors are those who give one or two ratings. Claims are made in the *Business Week* article that companies using this metric have found correlations between willingness to recommend and revenue.

What is attractive about this metric is *its simplicity*. But what is problematic about it is that it is still based on *soft, subjective data* that is collected at a point in time. For example, if you asked me about my willingness to recommend my broker on a given day, my ratings might

---

1. *Business Week*, January 30, 2006 issue.

have a lot to do with my portfolio's performance that day. Similarly, my willingness to recommend a hotel chain is heavily influenced by my last overnight stay and fading memory. And if a car company calls me on the day the "check engine" light came on in my car for the third time, my "willingness to recommend" score would be vastly different than if the call came a few weeks before the light ever came on.

The bottom line is that this metric is based on a survey. Surveys measure people's *perceptions* and what they *think*. But what people *say and do* are often quite different. For example, I recently rented a Kia Amanti and was extremely impressed with the comfort, acceleration, sound system, styling, and value. It has the feel of a $50,000 car and costs less than half that. I would be a "10" on the "willingness to rec-ommend" scale for the Amanti. But I would never buy one and give up my classic English car. So, my willingness-to-recommend score of "10" would not put a single dollar in Kia's bank account.

Some organizations are so excited about this one-question survey approach for customers that they have extended it to employees as well. For example, Caterpillar Financial Services (CFS) surveys its employees with a number of questions, but it really pays attention only to the last question on the survey, which asks about employees' willingness to recommend CFS as a great place to work.

Similarly, a manufacturing client recently explained to me that it used to use an expensive but well-researched set of 12 questions on an employee morale survey it did once a year. Now, the company just asks employees to answer the willingness-to-recommend question. Although the company is doing the survey once a month with a sam-ple of employees (which is vastly superior to an *annual* metric), it is still conducting a survey, and the survey consists of only one question. If the willingness-to-recommend response goes down, the company has no idea why—or what to do about it. A survey done on a particu-larly bad day may skew the results for that entire month.

This is not to suggest that there is something wrong with the one-question customer or employee survey. It is merely a reminder that such a survey should be one of a number of metrics that measure cus-tomer or employee satisfaction—not the *only* one! Measuring some-thing as important and complex as customer satisfaction or employee satisfaction based on how people answer one question is a huge risk.

The Lure of Simplicity

The problem with all of the metrics previously described is that *a single measure does not provide enough information either to tell an organization how it is really performing or to diagnose the causes of decline in performance.* If willingness to recommend goes down, or cost of quality goes up, do you know why and what to do about it? What about traditional metrics, such as sales? Even trying to determine why sales goals were not met can involve a lot of additional data gathering.

It is easy to understand the allure of the simple new metrics. Work would be much easier if we could just pay attention to a couple of charts—like watching the speedometer and gas gauge while driving. Indeed, the biggest appeal of the balanced scorecard approach is its simplicity. Running even a small organization, however, is quite a complex task and requires something more.

One of the most important lessons from Kaplan and Norton's book, *The Balanced Scorecard* (1996), and the 2004 APQC study is that fewer measures are better. In fact, both recommend using around 12 to 16 metrics. However, the tradeoff for this simpler way of running an organization is that important measures and facts may be ignored if they are not part of the 16 metrics on the scorecard.

Trying to run a complex business by looking at a few simplistic statistics is just as risky as routinely looking at 50 charts. Running a business requires collecting and reviewing *a wide variety of financial data,* and only a complete idiot would look at just one number, such as sales or growth. Yet many otherwise intelligent executives are willing to review a single measure like "willingness to recommend" as the only measure of customer satisfaction.

Going back to scorecards with 50 or more measures is not the answer either. The five companies selected by APQC as having the best scorecards in the United States, for example, use Stage III scorecards. All of the metrics are individual measures of a singular aspect of performance. Their managers and executives sit in meetings every month looking at spreadsheets and PowerPoint charts of performance statistics that are mostly lagging measures of company performance. But complex dimensions of performance—such as financial health, employee morale, risk, safety, or customer satisfaction—*cannot be mea-*

sured using a couple of simple statistics such as sales, accidents, a single survey question, or employee turnover.

The more we try to simplify our corporate scorecards, the less real business intelligence they provide. Buying the latest BI software is not the answer either. It is only as good as the metrics and data you put into it, and there are some BI systems with some pretty flawed metrics in them. *The best answer to finding the proper balance between complexity and simplicity is analytics.*

What Are Analytics?

Analytics are gauges on the organizational dashboard that tell leaders and managers how the organization is performing. Analytics are numbers, statistics, or metrics, but they are different from the metrics that make up most corporate scorecards. Analytics focus on a particular aspect of performance and are made up of a series of sub-metrics, each of which tracks a different dimension of your performance. Each sub-metric in a single analytic is assigned a weight depending on its importance, integrity, and credibility.

Based on this definition, gross margin would not be an analytic, even though it is made up of sales and expenses, and expenses can be further divided into labor, materials, and other sub-categories of costs. All of the sub-metrics that make up gross margin are measures of dollars. **In contrast, an analytic is a metric made up of sub-metrics that are** *different variables* **and often units of measurement**. A sub-measure might be given a higher weight if it is thought to be a stronger indicator of performance than other metrics in the analytic.

Examples of Analytics

Probably the easiest way to understand what an analytic is and how it differs from traditional organizational performance measures is to begin with a personal example. Let's say you wanted to create a simple analytic that provided an answer to the question "How healthy am I?" One choice would be to measure only your cholesterol, but that one number would hardly provide a complete picture of your health. For argument's sake, it might be useful to include five dimensions of health in this analytic and attempt to create a balance of leading and lagging sub-metrics. The dimensions shown in Figure 2-1 will be included in our health analytic and are weighted based on their importance.

Figure 2-1. Example Health Analytic

Each of the five sub-metrics in the health analytic would then drill down to tier three metrics. For example, the lifestyle metric might be composed of measures of diet, sleep, exercise, and stress. Blood chemistry metrics like cholesterol, triglycerides, and other factors are given the highest weight of all the sub-measures because they are the strongest determinant of health and longevity. Heredity is an important factor, but is also a lagging measure that nothing can be done about—you can't change who your parents are or were.

Lifestyle is the most forward looking of the sub-metrics and the one you have the most influence over, because it boils down to measures of behavior. In fact, lifestyle changes such as diet, exercise, vitamins, and prescription drugs can have a positive impact on body composition, blood chemistry, and vitals like blood pressure and resting heart rate. Lifestyle metrics, however, are the measures with the least integrity. People tend to overestimate how much they exercise and underestimate how much they eat. Measures of body composition, blood chemistry, and vitals have excellent integrity because they are obtained by an outside third party using equipment designed to measure these factors.

Now, let's look at a business example. Let's say we wanted to construct an index or analytic of an organization's financial health. The financial health analytic might contain the dimensions of performance shown in Figure 2-2.

This financial analytic is well balanced because it includes measures of the past (gross margin), present (accounts receivable and assets/liabilities), and future (orders/proposals). Just like heredity in

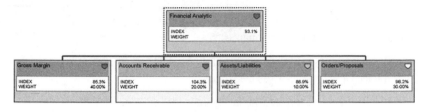

Figure 2-2. Example Financial Analytic

the health example above, gross margin is a very important and highly weighted metric, but you can't do anything this month about *last* month's gross margin. Of these four sub-metrics, the one that can be influenced the most is orders and proposals. This metric drives sales and cash flow, and it should help increase assets.

Characteristics of an Analytic

Analytics have certain characteristics that separate them from traditional performance metrics: Figure 2-3 lists these.

Why Analytics Are Superior to Singular Metrics

Analytics are better than singular metrics because ***they provide a better overall assessment of a dimension of performance than a single measure of one performance factor***. For example, you would never evaluate how your car is performing by measuring just the oil pressure. And you would never evaluate your health by assessing only your blood pressure.

Similarly, an organization cannot evaluate something as complicated as customer satisfaction or product quality by collecting data on a single measure. The alternative of measuring 50 or 60 different things is not feasible either. Analytics provide a more balanced and thorough assessment of performance because they are based on 3 to 6 individual metrics of different performance dimensions that are each weighted. A scorecard that includes 16 analytics may be made up of more than 100 sub-measures, but these sub-measures are stacked in tiers so that one needs to drill down to the detailed measures only when there is a problem.

1. Each individual analytic provides data on an important question about organizational health or performance.

2. A scorecard or dashboard for an organization would consist of 12 to 20 analytics that roll up into 4 to 6 high-level analytics.

3. Analytics always comprise lower-level metrics or "drill-downs."

4. Analytics require targets or objectives before they become meaningful.

5. Each sub-metric is a discrete measure, not just the same measure broken down in further detail.

6. Correlations between discrete analytics can be determined with time and experimentation, allowing leaders to forecast future performance better and allocate resources more intelligently.

7. Analytics do not take the place of experience, observation, and anecdotal data gathered by being in touch with the operation.

8. Analytics provide data to assess each and every improvement initiative and strategy in the company.

9. To be useful, analytics require software tools, but even small companies can afford these tools.

10. Analytics change and improve each year as the organization gathers more data, learns more important lessons, and its people become more sophisticated with regard to measuring and analyzing performance.

Figure 2-3. Characteristics of an Analytic

Some Disadvantages of a Scorecard Based on Analytics

The only real disadvantage of a scorecard that includes several analytic metrics is that it is initially complicated and difficult for people to interpret. It will take a while for some people to become accustomed to looking at an analytic and understanding what goes into it. Some will automatically want to drill down to the lower-level sub-measures each time, just so they can remember what makes up the analytic. Others will learn to trust the warning light that goes with the display of each analytic. Detail-oriented technical types (such as engineers, accountants, and scientists) tend to love analytics and immediately grasp the inherent logic in looking at one summary metric that incorporates several individual measures of performance. Others will hate this complexity and will always prefer looking at a couple of individual performance measures that they have trusted in the past. The way to get these types of individuals to buy into the analytics scorecard is to show them that their favorite metrics are still probably on the scorecard; they just are two or three levels below the summary analytic.

For example, someone in one of my workshops recently critiqued a scorecard built around analytics: "There are really over 75 measures on the scorecard because each of the 15 analytics is made up of 2 to 5 submetrics, and some of those are made up of even lower level metrics." This is a true statement. However, the CEO scorecard had 15 metrics. If all 15 were green and there were no idiot lights showing red or yellow, there is absolutely no reason to drill down into the tier two or three submetrics. Without these lower layers of data, however, it is impossible to determine the location of problems and diagnose their causes.

> *A scorecard based around analytics simply provides a more complete assessment of performance than does one based around individual measures.*

How Analytics Change the Way an Organization Reviews Performance

The first big change you will notice is that you don't have to work overtime each month preparing charts for presentation at those dreaded monthly review meetings. PowerPoint charts and spreadsheet presentations are not used to present data on analytics. Instead, someone brings a laptop to the meeting room, signs on to the company's database of performance analytics, and displays real-time performance for everyone to see. If one of the analytics is showing yellow (which means marginal) or red (which means trouble), the owner of that analytic can drill down into the sub-measures as far as necessary to determine why the overall analytic is red or yellow and what is being done to correct it. The labor saved in not having to prepare for monthly meetings anymore often more than pays for the scorecard software in a single year.

Something else that you will notice is that it becomes increasingly difficult for employees to manipulate scores on performance measures. When organizations focus on a singular metric, employees often learn how to make performance on that metric look good, but often at the expense of other aspects of performance. A good balanced scorecard is supposed to take care of this but often does not. Analytics make it more likely to drive desired behavior and priorities in an organization and are less subject to manipulation or cheating.

A Scorecard Can Include Both Analytics and Singular Metrics

Combining analytics and singular metrics on a scorecard is probably the best way of introducing the concepts of analytics in an organization. Your first version of an analytics scorecard might include 12 individual metrics and 4 analytics; over time (e.g., 3 to 5 years), you may work up to having a scorecard that uses only analytics as metrics.

Deciding how long to spend phasing in this new approach to measurement has a lot to do with an organization's performance and willingness to accept change. For example, a company that is in big trouble might need to implement an analytics-based scorecard very quickly to drive behavior and survive, whereas a successful organization that is feeling no threats can have the luxury of phasing this approach in over several years.

The section of your scorecard that is most likely to have singular metrics is the financial one. Many high-level financial statistics like profit, EBITDA or gross margin, are aggregates of many other numbers, but they are not true analytics, because all numbers are a measure of dollars.

Performance Dimensions That Are Best Suited to Analytics

The best types of performance dimensions for analytics are complicated attributes of an organization that are impossible to assess by looking at one or two numbers. For example, the financial health of an organization is determined by looking at a wide variety of factors. When analysts try to predict the future performance of a company, they study a wide range of financial statistics and ratios to determine the current and future health of the enterprise.

Employee satisfaction is also a dimension of performance that would be difficult to evaluate using one or two statistics, such as turnover. Something like productivity of labor, milestones met on a big project, or cost reduction are performance aspects that might be measured using a single metric versus an analytic.

A singular metric might also be appropriate for an objective measure linked to important customer or stakeholder requirements, like on-time landings for an airline or repairs done correctly by maintenance technicians.

How Data Is Displayed in an Analytic

Analytics are always displayed as a score from 0 to 100, with 100 showing the best performance. This is a scale that everyone understands, and it includes sufficient width to allow for a wide range of performance. One of the beauties of an analytic is that it allows you to combine unlike units of measurement. For example, you might have three separate metrics in an analytic for an IT help desk's customer satisfaction analytic:

1. Cycle time for responding to help/problems (measured in minutes)
2. Trouble tickets cleared in 24 hours or less (measured in percent)
3. Customer satisfaction scores gathered via telephone survey (measured in average rating on a 1 to 5 scale)

To combine these three related but dissimilar units of measurement into a single analytic, performance needs to be converted to multiples of 10 on a 100-point scale. For example, a score of 4 on a 5-point sale survey would equate to 80. Chapter 3 offers details on how to construct and calculate performance using an analytic metric.

Analytics Can Be Used to Hide Confidential Information

Not every organization wants to reveal all of its numbers to all employees and partners. At the same time, there is a need to communicate with people how the organization is performing. Using analytics facilitates sharing information that should be shared while protecting information that should remain undisclosed.

For example, a privately owned construction company client has found that the analytics on its scorecard allow the company to communicate such sensitive financial measures as profits, ROI, and sales without revealing the actual numbers. Instead, all gauges are shown in multiples of 0 to 10 with high values being better. By looking at performance this way, all employees can monitor how the company is performing against its goals and targets without seeing sensitive information that might make its way into the hands of competitors. The company uses a cool graphic to display the data it call its dashboard, and it looks like the dashboard of a Ferrari. And the company has found that its employees have no trouble understanding the data displayed in analytics this way.

Analytics Allow You to Use Many of Your Existing Metrics

One of the easiest ways of convincing people to adopt a scorecard based on analytics is to show them that all their favorite metrics can still be used. They may go from being a tier-one measure to being a tier-three metric, but there is room for them as sub-metrics in an analytic. So if your CEO is enamored with the new "willingness-to-recommend" customer survey, include it as a sub-metric. Or if you want to continue measuring on-time delivery or Six Sigma project successes, include these measures in one of your analytics.

Analytics do not involve adding more measures to your scorecard. Rather, they allow you to stack your metrics in layers that can be drilled into when necessary. If the overall analytic or summary gauge shows green, and there are no warning lights on to indicate a problem with one of the sub-metrics, there is no need to drill down into the detail. This allows leaders to spend time on aspects of the organization that do need their attention.

3

The Analytics-Based Scorecard: Adding More Business Intelligence to Your Metrics

---

The scorecards used by many organizations today are characterized by a lack of attention to detail and often miss many important aspects of performance. This chapter describes how to construct a better scorecard architecture and provides guidelines that will help make the metrics on your scorecard tell leaders as much as possible about organizational performance.

Don't Just Blindly Follow a Template: Create *Your Own* Scorecard

In the last 15 years, I have helped many corporations and government organizations design scorecards. One major lesson I learned during this process is that blindly following a scorecard template presented in a book does not work very well. Some of the best scorecards I have seen do not include the ubiquitous four categories defined by Kaplan and Norton: financial, customer, internal, and innovation/growth. Although these four categories are a good starting point, it is best to change and adapt this architecture to what fits your organization.

Kaplan and Norton were the pioneers of the concept of a balanced scorecard, and their approach to scorecard design is more than 15 years old. Obviously, the field of performance management has evolved over the last decade and a half, and scorecard models must follow suit. Since 1996, the year *Keeping Score* was published, my own views on performance measurement have changed quite a bit. One of the lessons learned during this time is that most metrics should not be derived from an organization's vision but should be linked, instead, to an organization's mission (i.e., its reason for existing).

Another lesson learned was that Kaplan and Norton's model is not necessarily the best template for all organizations to follow; an alternative, commonly used scorecard architecture follows the six categories of "Business Results" in the Baldrige Award model:

1. Product/service quality
2. Customer focus
3. Finance and market
4. Human resources
5. Organizational effectiveness
6. Leadership/social responsibility

In some ways (and for some organizations), the Baldrige architecture is superior to Kaplan and Norton's because it includes a category for people or human resource metrics. In today's organizations, people are a major expense, but they can also be a major competitive advantage in companies such as Google and Microsoft. The last category of data in the Baldrige model, leadership/social responsibility, is also attractive because it gives you a place to put the strategic metrics tied to your vision and strategy and a place to incorporate measures of ethics, regulatory compliance, and social responsibility. None of these items fit neatly in any of the four categories in Kaplan and Norton's model, and this alone reflects the need for a more relevant scorecard architecture. In the last few years, we have learned that measures of ethics and social responsibility can just as easily bring a company to its knees as poor financial results can. In spite of this, many organizations have no metrics directly concerned with ethics and social responsibility; they compensate for this by putting ethics under training attendance and compliance with Sarbanes-Oxley.

A New Scorecard Architecture

Although there is probably no such thing as an ideal scorecard architecture that fits all types of organizations, a contemporary scorecard must reflect current realities. For this reason, it makes sense to consider adding a couple of new categories of data to enhance older models. The new straw man model that I encourage my clients to start with includes the following categories:

1. External Metrics
2. Customer Metrics
3. People Metrics
4. Internal Metrics
5. Financial and Strategic Metrics

All types of organizations need to consider the first four categories of metrics presented here because all organizations, even government and nonprofit organizations, have external factors they need to monitor. They also need metrics that look at how they are doing with customers, employees, and internal measures of things like quality, productivity, and process consistency.

The fifth category of metrics—financial and strategic metrics—is critical for all business organizations that need to also monitor financial results, but an entire category devoted to financial measures may not be as critical to government or nonprofit organizations. It also makes sense to separate the strategic measures (vision) from operational or mission-related measures. Because strategic measures are often financial in nature, it makes sense to pair them with financial metrics. If that section of your scorecard is too crowded, you might consider creating a separate category for your strategic metrics. One option is to put vision-related metrics at the top of your executive scorecard.

The categories that you select for your scorecard architecture, whether your scorecard is based on singular metrics or analytics, are not necessarily different. If you are happy with the four categories on your current scorecard, stick with them. You can make the transition from singular metrics to analytics an evolutionary process, and this process will occur no matter which categories of data you choose for your scorecard. And while it is rare to see a Stage IV scorecard that consists entirely of analytics, most of the metrics will be.

Oddly enough, as scorecards cascade down from executives to lower-level employees, you will find fewer analytics and more singular metrics. The reason for this is that executives need to have a broad view of organizational performance, so they need broad metrics that include a variety of health factors. As you move down the organizational chart to department managers, supervisors, and individual workers, the number of metrics on the scorecard become fewer, and the number of analytics become fewer as well. Worker scorecards often include 4 to 6 metrics, with only 1 or 2 analytics among them.

What Managers Need to Know About Performance

There are four basic facts that a manager or employee needs to know about each measure of performance. These are presented below in a Q & A format:

- **What is the current level of performance?** *Level* is defined as how current performance compares to a target or objective and is usually displayed as red, yellow, or green. Performance levels may also be compared to historical data (such as what occurred last year or last quarter) or to other units in the organization.
- **What is the trend?** *Trend* is defined as performance over time. Trend is an important dimension of performance and is just as important as the current performance or level, which is just a single data point. Trends show improving, declining, or flat levels of performance over time.
- **Analysis: Why is this level and trend in performance occurring?** This is qualitative information that explains the quantitative level and trend. The explanation of the root cause of problems or declines should be included. It may also be important to document the reasons or causes for good (green) performance or an improving trend.
- **Action plan: What is being done to improve performance or maintain it at current levels?** The action plan usually consists of a series of tasks, responsibilities, and deadlines. It is important that action plans are

derived from the analysis information. The owner of the metric is usually responsible for developing the action plan.

An example of data displayed using this format appears in Figure 3-1.

If your scorecard software or performance reporting system does not display these four quadrants of information about each measure, you are missing some important information. In any briefing meeting where performance is being discussed, leaders should be taught to ask about *level, trend, analysis,* and *action plan* for every measure that gets reviewed.

Flying Blind: What's Missing from Most Scorecards

The *categories* of measures on your scorecard are nowhere near as important as the *metrics* themselves and the *integrity* of the data collected. The categories are just a sorting mechanism; so if you like the Kaplan and Norton model, or some other approach, just stick with it. Spend your time debating and thinking about which metrics belong in which category, not what the categories are. The metrics matter so much because they are used to obtain important information. If they are not well defined, the information will not be forthcoming. When this occurs, managers are, in a sense, flying blind, because their scorecards provide only a partial picture of the health of the organization and crucial data goes missing.

Figure 3-2 is a checklist of information that most leaders do not see when looking at their scorecards. Use this checklist as a resource when thinking about how much your scorecards reveal (or fail to reveal) about your own organization's performance.

It is safe to bet that most leaders and managers reading the list in Figure 3-2 would want to have quantifiable answers to all the questions above. Sadly, *most scorecards do not provide data on any of these things.* Or, even worse, they *purport* to provide data, but *they are false and inaccurate indicators of what is really going on.* It is, in fact, better to have no hard data at all than a metric that lacks integrity. The false or

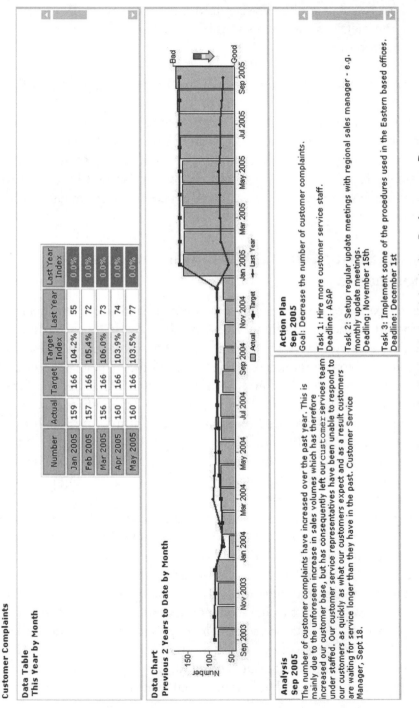

Customer Complaints

Data Table
This Year by Month

Number	Actual	Target	Target Index	Last Year	Last Year Index
Jan 2005	159	166	104.2%	55	0.0%
Feb 2005	157	166	105.4%	72	0.0%
Mar 2005	156	166	106.0%	73	0.0%
Apr 2005	160	166	103.9%	74	0.0%
May 2005	160	166	103.5%	77	0.0%

Data Chart
Previous 2 Years to Date by Month

Actual   Target   Last Year

Analysis
Sep 2005
The number of customer complaints have increased over the past year. This is mainly due to the unforeseen increase in sales volumes which has therefore increased our customer base, but has consequently left our customer services team under staffed. Our customer service representatives have been unable to respond to our customers as quickly as what our customers expect and as a result customers are waiting for service longer than they have in the past. Customer Service Manager, Sept 18.

Action Plan
Sep 2005
Goal: Decrease the number of customer complaints.

Task 1: Hire more customer service staff.
Deadline: ASAP

Task 2: Setup regular update meetings with regional sales manager - e.g. monthly update meetings.
Deadline: November 15th

Task 3: Implement some of the procedures used in the Eastern based offices.
Deadline: December 1st

Figure 3-1. Example Screen for Reviewing and Analyzing Performance Data

Do They Provide This Information?

Customer Information

1. How hard is it for customers to do business with our firm, and how much do we irritate or frustrate them?
2. Who are our most profitable and important customers, and where do we stand in our relationships with them?
3. Are any of our important customers looking around for another supplier or using one already?
4. Do we have any customers that we would be better off without?

Employee Information

5. How much do we irritate our employees and make them frustrated or unhappy?
6. Is our corporate culture still positive, and do people really live by the values we have on the walls?
7. How well are we communicating important information to our employees and other partners?
8. Do we have the right people in the right jobs, and do they have the knowledge and skills we need for today and tomorrow's work?
9. How much time do our employees spend each day doing what we hired them to do?
10. Are our employees and leaders ethical and honest?
11. How are we really doing on diversity?
12. How safe is it to work in this organization?
13. How healthy are the executives and employees who work in this company?

External Information

14. How healthy are the relationships we have with our most important partners and suppliers?
15. How strong is our brand image in the marketplace?
16. At what level of risk is our organization for some type of threat or disaster?
17. How are we doing at meeting regulatory and legal requirements?
18. What sort of competitive threats and other risks are we facing and how well have we prepared for these risks?

Financial Information

19. How are we doing on our major capital projects?
20. Are we going after the right types of new business?
21. What are financial results going to look like a few months from now?
22. How are we doing at coming up with new products and services that the market embraces?
23. Are the investments we've made in performance improvement initiatives or products really paying off?

Figure 3-2. Questions to Ask About Your Organization's Scorecards

inaccurate data produced by such a metric may lull executives into a false sense of security when they should be concerned.

What Most Scorecards Really Tell Leaders

Most scorecards really tell leaders the type of information listed in Figure 3-3. The contrast between the figures is telling and should serve as a cautionary note. Moreover, it is important to note that the metrics listed in Figure 3-3 are typical in organizations that claim they have a balanced scorecard.

The problem with the list in Figure 3-3 is that almost all the measures are either lagging metrics or metrics that *lack integrity*. The bottom line is that most scorecards don't even come close to telling managers and leaders what they need to know to run a department, unit, or entire enterprise. The measures they are looking at are only a portion of the information really needed to make decisions and develop strategies. Furthermore, most of the measures are of things that have already happened. This is the *least* important type of data to review.

External Factors: What to Include on This Section of Your Scorecard

In the past, I always advised clients not to include external factors on their scorecards. The premise behind this was that the scorecard should include measures of the client organization's performance and that each metric should be a factor that the organization can exert a fair degree of influence on to move performance. Over the last few years, however, I have come to realize that *external factors should be included as a category of data on a good balanced scorecard* and that this might include metrics that *you have no influence or control over* but that are nevertheless linked to your success.

For example, if you are in the airline business, the price of fuel is not something you can do much about, but it certainly has a huge impact on your profits. Similarly, if you are in the car business and 40 percent of your revenue comes from SUVs, the price of gasoline will also have a huge impact on your sales and profits. As the price of gas

Financial Information

1. How profitable were we last month or quarter?

2. What were our sales and expenses last month or quarter?

3. How much did we grow in sales and profits from last year?

4. What's our stock price or budget?

5. What is the productivity of our labor/equipment/capital?

Customer Information

6. How do the minority of customers who bother to fill out our surveys rate us?

7. How many lost customers did we have last month or quarter?

8. How many customer complaints did we receive last month?

9. How much repeat business did we get from existing customers?

Employee Information

10. How do employees rate their satisfaction with their jobs on the one day a year we do a survey?

11. How many hours did employees spend sitting in training classes last month/year?

12. What is our percentage of employee turnover?

13. How many lost-time accidents did we have and what did it cost us?

Productivity Information

14. How are we doing on operational measures unique to our industry?

15. How many defective products or services got produced?

16. How many late deliveries did we have?

Figure 3-3. What Most Scorecards Really Tell Leaders

creeps up to $5 per gallon, those big Expeditions and Hummers don't look quite so attractive.

Prices aren't the only external factor, of course: Consumer trends can also have a big positive or negative impact on your business. For example, McDonalds was the pioneer in canceling "Supersize" items on its menu after the movie *Supersize Me* was released. Public sentiment that fast-food companies could be held liable in court for making people fat and giving them health problems like diabetes was an additional incentive for change.

If you work in a government organization or sell to one, politics are an external factor that can certainly have a huge impact on your business and on many metrics on your scorecard. You can bet that defense companies are tracking conflicts around the world and public opinions about war, terrorism, and other factors that might affect their sales and profits.

As the examples cited above illustrate, it makes sense to include a section on external metrics on your scorecard so that all important information a manager needs is in one spot. You have little or no influence over external factors such as the economy, interest rates, or world events, but other factors, such as politics, brand image, regulations, and competitive threats, *can* be influenced.

Customer Measures: What to Include on This Section of Your Scorecard

The design of this section of your scorecard has a lot to do with the type of organization you have and the different customers you serve. For example, the Workforce Development Division in the City of Los Angeles helps find disadvantaged people jobs and helps employers in the city find people to fill open jobs. The factors that are important to these two customer groups are very different, so it made sense for this organization to develop two different customer metrics on its scorecard: one for job seekers and one for employers. The metrics include both hard measures (such as pay, turnover, and working conditions) and soft measures (such as job satisfaction gathered via interviews and surveys).

This section of the scorecard should provide you with the following information:

- How are we doing at marketing and sales to bring in new customers?
- How are we doing at taking care of existing customers?
- What are we doing to manage and build strong relationships with our important customers?

Traditional customer metrics like the dollar value of a new business, customer spending, surveys, and complaints do not really provide a clear picture of how an organization is doing at serving its customers. Business is about relationships, and most organizations have no idea about the health of the relationships they have with customers.

People Measures: What to Include in This Section of Your Scorecard

A client in the home-building business recently explained that employee satisfaction and engagement is his #1 business concern. The reason for this is that housing starts are double what they were a few years ago in the marketplace he serves (Phoenix), and finding and keeping good people is a major challenge. For this client as for other business executives, turnover is a sobering metric, one that cannot be improved after someone leaves. Employee surveys do not have much of an impact on turnover and tend to be a waste of time because people are often not honest, and a survey measures morale only on the day it is administered. Because people are critical to all businesses, the metrics used to measure "people factors" should be the same in just about any type of organization. This section of the scorecard should tell leaders:

- Are employees happy and engaged in their jobs?
- Are they healthy and safe at work?
- How are we really doing on ethics and diversity?
- Do we have the right people with the right skills for today and tomorrow's work?
- Are we effectively communicating with our employees and other key partners?

Organizations like Google pride themselves on being a great place to work, but as the company continues to grow quickly and hire several hundred new people a month, it becomes harder and harder to maintain the culture the company started with. The people measures on the scorecard help tell leaders if the culture is still positive as the organization goes through cycles of change and growth or decline.

Operational Measures: What to Include on This Section of Your Scorecard

This section of the scorecard, unlike the previous section, is most likely to be *unique*, depending on the type of industry you are in. All industries have standard metrics that everyone tracks, such as "comebacks" in the auto maintenance business or average speed to answer in a call center. This is the section of the scorecard where all those industry-specific metrics go. The challenge in this section is to narrow down the data to a few summary analytics that focus on major performance dimensions, such as:

- product/service quality,
- productivity,
- timeliness, and
- creativity.

Analytics are an excellent way of collapsing a series of individual metrics into a single statistic that provides leaders with an overall view of performance. For example, hospital leaders used to review performance on more than 100 clinical quality metrics per month. Now, they look at one measure that is an analytic made up of the major measures of clinical quality. The individual metrics are grouped into additional analytics. One looks at those that address protection from infection, others address timely patient treatment, etc. With this data in place, hospital leaders can review one analytic metric that answers this question: How are we doing on all our clinical measures? If the overall measure shows yellow or red, if there is a downward trend, or if the warning light is on, hospital leaders drill down into the data to find out the problem.

Most of the analytics in the operational measures section tell leaders how an organization is performing its day-to-day responsibilities, producing products, or delivering services. Large organizations often spend some percentage of their resources on special projects as well. A project is an activity with a clear beginning and end that produces some sort of deliverable. For example, a project might be to construct a new plant, install a major software system, launch a new business unit, buy another company, or implement new technology or equipment.

The measures in this section of the scorecard should answer the following questions:

- How are we doing on our major projects?
- Are we consistently producing and delivering high quality products/services?
- Are we maximizing the productivity of our people and other major resources?
- Are the performance improvement initiatives we're working on really working?
- How are we doing at researching and developing new or improved products and services?

This section of the scorecard is also where you would put any measures of your key business processes. For example, some organizations prefer to look at performance in terms of *processes* rather than *output* such as products or services, so this would be the place to put those measures.

Strategic and Financial Measures: What to Include in This Section of Your Scorecard

This is the section of the scorecard where everyone wants to cram 20 to 30 measures. It is very hard for many leaders to conceptualize running their organizations by looking at only a handful of financial and strategic measures. Once they realize that their 20 to 30 individual statistics can be tiered into 3 to 4 high-level analytics, however, they are often willing to adopt this new approach to measuring financial results. Many executives begin the change process by looking three or four layers into the financial measures anyway, because they do not truly believe that that analytic will reveal important facts they need to be aware of. Eventually, these individuals begin to trust the integrity of the analytic and recognize that the warning light will show yellow or red, alerting them to drill down deeper into the data. Just about anything you want to know about the financial health of an organization can be found by answering the questions below:

- How are we doing on our major strategies or goals that link to our vision?
- Are we profitable and getting good return on investment?
- How's our market share?
- How's our cash flow?
- How do our future financial results look?
- Are we growing?

Building an Analytics-Based Scorecard

Creating an analytic metric is really quite a simple process. It is most often done with a team of people familiar with this aspect of performance in the organization. You don't want the team to get too large: 4 to 8 people is ideal. The approach is outlined in the following steps, using a personal health example that we can all relate to. The purpose of the analytic is to tell us about the health of our department of 420 people.

Step 1: Identify a Dimension of Performance for Focus

In our example, we are going to focus on your health. In an organization, dimensions focus on answering the questions outlined in the last few pages. For example, an organization might focus on the financial health of a company, or the safety of its people, or the relationships it has with customers. A dimension might also be a major process, such as R&D or sales.

Step 2: List All Current Metrics and Brainstorm Possible Metrics That Could Be Tracked

Team members begin by listing the existing data we have or could easily get. Next, brainstorm possible metrics that might go into this analytic. Caution people to not discuss or debate the ideas for metrics, just write them down. The team working on creating a health analytic brainstormed the health metrics listed in Figure 3-4.

Step 3: Narrow Down the Brainstormed List to a Vital Few Metrics

A quick way of getting everyone's input is to have each individual select the 6 measures in the list (in this case, in Figure 3-4) that they

☐ C-Reactive protein

☐ Blood pressure

☐ Resting heart rate

☐ HDL cholesterol

☐ LDL cholesterol

☐ Total cholesterol

☐ Triglycerides

☐ Weight

☐ BMI (body mass index)

☐ Blood sugar

☐ Waist size

☐ Family history

☐ Antioxidants

☐ Past illnesses and procedures

☐ Diagnostic test results (e.g., stress test, colonoscopy, mammogram)

☐ Frequency and completeness of physical checkups

☐ Frequency of doctor visits

☐ Existing problems/conditions and severity

☐ Exercise

☐ Diet

☐ Stress

☐ Driving factors (e.g., speed, traffic, seat belts, etc.)

☐ Smoking

☐ Dangerous hobbies

☐ Vitamins and supplements

Figure 3-4. Example of Possible and Existing Metrics for Assessing Health

think most reflect a person's overall health. Urge them to try to think of a mix of past, present, and future measures, and to also consider whether or not it is possible to gather the data. Also caution the team members to think about the *integrity* of the data. For example, diet might be a hugely important factor in a person's health, but getting people to remember what they ate and be honest about reporting it are two huge challenges. After tabulating all the votes of the team members, some themes emerge, showing which metrics most people thought were important; Figure 3-5 shows a more focused list of metrics:

History	Health Statistics	Lifestyle
Family history	Cholesterol	Diet
Personal history	Blood pressure	Exercise
	Blood chemistry	Stress/sleep
	Weight/height/age	Medication
	Cardiac health	Vitamins

Figure 3-5. A More Focused List of Health Metrics to Track

Step 4: Assign Weights to the Sub-Metrics That Will Make Up the Analytic

Our team acknowledged that heredity and history are important determinants of health, but nothing can be done about these things. The data with the highest integrity are the health statistics because those are measured using specialized devices and tests, and data are collected by doctors and lab technicians. The weights established by the team are shown in Figure 3-6.

History 15%		Health Statistics 50%		Lifestyle 35%	
Family history	40%	Cholesterol	20%	Diet	30%
Personal history	60%	Blood pressure	20%	Exercise	25%
		Cardiac health	20%	Medication	20%
		Blood chemistry	20%	Stress/sleep	15%
		Weight/height/age	20%	Vitamins	10%

Figure 3-6. A Weighted List of Sample Health Metrics

Step 5: Complete Metric Definition Sheets for Each of the Individual Metrics and Analytics That Make Up the High-Level Analytic

It is best to start this process with the lowest level of metric that will be part of the analytic. In the health example, we may decide to begin with blood pressure. Some of the questions you need to answer regarding this metric are listed in Figure 3-7.

---

1. What is the purpose of this metric—i.e., what behavior is this expected to drive?

2. What is the definition of this metric?

3. What type of metric is this? (e.g., single measure, analytic/index, ratio).

4. What is the unit of measure that will be used and expected scale?

5. What is the formula for calculating this metric?

6. How often will data be collected on this metric?

7. What data collection method will be used?

8. Does the data exist on this metric? (Yes, No, Somewhat)

9. Does historical data exist on this metric?

10. Who is the owner of this metric?

11. Who will be responsible for collecting the data?

12. Have targets (e.g., red, yellow, green) been set for this metric?

13. What is the desired polarity for this metric?
    - Higher is better
    - Lower is better
    - In the middle is better

Figure 3-7. Questions to Ask When Developing Metrics

Step 6: Develop Data Collection Plans, Instruments, and Procedures

Once you have defined the metrics in Step 5, you now need to figure out how to gather the data. This is often one of the biggest challenges of a scorecard project. Often, the metrics get revised or even deleted once you sit down and figure out how much work and expense is required to gather the data. This step often requires many months to complete if the analytic consists of many new metrics. Data collection plans include a list of deliverables and their specifications (e.g., a 1-page survey with 10–12 questions). Data collection plans also include a list of tasks, responsibilities, and deadlines as with any project.

(*Note*: You can skip this step if data exists for all the individual metrics in the analytic. However, this is rarely the case.)

Step 7: Collect Baseline Data or Gather Historical Data on All the Individual Metrics that Make Up the Analytic

The next step is to collect historical data on each of the individual metrics that make up the analytic, or, if none exist, to gather some baseline data. For the sake of our example, this might involve getting all employees to go in for a blood test and physical to get baseline data on all the health statistics in our analytic. Data on family history and lifestyle factors might be gathered via a single survey. There are a number of good ones out there, such as the one at realeage.com that looks at a variety of factors to determine your physical age versus your chronological age. Various factors in the survey make you either younger than your years (e.g., regular exercise, good sleep, wearing seat belts) or older than your years (e.g., smoking, bad diet, and dangerous sports/hobbies).

Step 8: Establish Red, Yellow, and Green Targets or Ranges

Once you have some baseline data and hopefully some data from other organizations, you can begin to set values for red, yellow, and green. Targets should be based on your own history or baseline, benchmarks, industry averages, your own best performance, and specific competitors. In our example of health statistics, there is plenty of data derived from research on what "green" should look like. For example, for total cholesterol, you might define the targets as follows:

Green   = 150 or below
Yellow = 151–200
Red   = Greater than 200

Targets need to be set for each individual metric that will make up the analytic, and they should never be set arbitrarily. If you have no historical data, let a small group of experts reach consensus on what red, yellow, and green values look like. You can always adjust the targets later as you get more data points.

Step 9: Establish Values for Expected Range of Performance on All Sub-Metrics

The purpose of this step is to set up a scale to convert performance data on different units of measurement into multiples of 10 so they can later be combined into an analytic that looks at overall performance. It is helpful to use a scale that goes from a low of 30 to a high of 120. If you have data on what good and poor levels of performance are, it is easy to establish the values along the scale. If the metric is new and you have no normative or comparative data, you have to estimate baseline at around 30 and your target at around 80 and then complete the scale.

Figure 3-8 illustrates the cholesterol metric we have been using, and Figure 3-10 is the worksheet for a complete analytic that is made up of four sub-metrics.

Measure	Scale															Wt. Score
	-30	-20	-10	0	10	20	30	40	50	60	70	80	90	100	110	120
Total mg. Cholesterol	>340	320	300	280	260	240	220	200	180	160	140	120	100	80	60	<60

Figure 3-8. Sample Cholesterol Metric

The scale shown in Figure 3-8 is entered into the scorecard software so that when data is entered, it is automatically translated into a value on our scale. For example:

- a cholesterol reading of 160 would get a score of 60,
- a reading of 250 would translate to a 15, and
- a reading of 100 would get a 90.

If we averaged these three readings, it would come to 170, which would translate to a 55 on the scale shown in Figure 3-8. The same process is repeated for each of the sub-metrics in an analytic, so that all expected performance levels can be translated into a multiple of 10 on the scale.

The next example illustrates an Employee Satisfaction Analytic in a call center that is made up of the sub-metrics and weights shown in Figure 3-9.

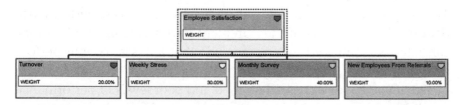

Figure 3-9. Example of Sub-Metrics for an Employee Satisfaction Analytic

Once the values are entered into the software as a formula for converting raw data to a multiple of 10, this function is performed automatically by the software. In other words, the software will take the raw data that is either hand entered or pulled from an existing database and will translate it into the analytic for the scorecard. Where necessary, the user can also view the raw data to see the absolute values of the sub-metric.

Measure	Scale	Wt. Score
	-30 -20 -10 0 10 20 30 40 50 60 70 80 90 100 110 120	
Total mg.	>340 320 300 280 260 240 220 200 180 160 140 120 100 80 60 <60	
Turnover %	>100 95 90 85 80 75 70 65 60 55 40 35 30 25 20 <20	20%
Weekly % Green (Stress)	<5 10 15 20 25 30 35 40 50 56 62 68 74 80 86 >92	30%
Survey % + Ratings	<5 10 15 20 25 30 35 40 50 56 62 68 74 80 86 >92	40%
New EEs From Referrals	0 3 6 9 12 15 18 21 25 28 31 34 37 40 43 >47	10%

Figure 3-10. Employee Satisfaction Analytic

Using the scale shown in Figure 3-10, let's say we had the following performance for the month of June:

Turnover	= 62% = 50 × 20% (wt) =	10
Weekly Stress	= 25% = 25 × 30% (wt) =	7.5
Survey Ratings	= 70% = 80 × 40% (wt) =	32
Referrals	= 30% = 70 × 10% (wt) =	7
Total		56.5/100
		Yellow

If we drilled down into the details of our 56.5, score we would find out that the metric that is most driving the analytic into the yellow is the *weekly stress* measure: This measure is in the red zone. Based on this, we would drill down further on the stress metric to see if it is coming from a particular location, shift, or department in the organization and then gather additional data to find out the root cause. That information would then be documented in the "Analysis" section of the scorecard software, and an "Action Plan" would be created to reduce the level of stress in the work environment.

Software Requirements for an Analytics Scorecard

There are some excellent software programs on the market for collecting, reporting, and analyzing data in a scorecard populated with analytics data. There are a number of things that are important when considering scorecard software. One of the most important factors is ease of use. Many organizations fail to use the expensive scorecard software they purchase because it is too complicated, and people prefer using good old PowerPoint charts and spreadsheets.

Factors such as ease of use, flexibility, linkages to other data and systems, and cost are all a matter of degree. The three requirements discussed here, however, are black and white. In other words, if the software does not have all three of these features, *do not buy it. It is not suited to a scorecard built around analytics.* Good scorecard software must have the following features:

Requirement #1: Warning or Idiot Lights for Each Metric

Using software that does not have the warning light feature for each metric is very dangerous. The warning lights tell managers that even though performance may show green on the overall analytic, one of the sub-metrics is yellow or red, and the manager should drill down into the data to find out which one and why.

Remember that an analytic is a *summary* of several different individual measures or factors. Good performance on two of the sub-metrics could have a lot of power in making the overall analytic metric green. However, a good manager wants to know about little tumors in the organization before they become inoperable, so the warning lights serve the purpose of identifying smaller problems and their locations.

There are a number of business intelligence and scorecard software programs that do not have this warning light feature built in. Cross those off your list.

Requirement #2: Unlimited Scorecard Architecture

Whatever scorecard software is used, do not select one that forces you into textbook scorecard architecture. Kaplan and Norton's four categories fit some organizations well, but not others. The Baldrige 6 results categories work for some, but not others.

Whatever scorecard software you use, make sure that it allows you to design the scorecard categories around the architectural model of your choosing. It is important to understand that the architecture of a scorecard tends to change with time, as organizations become more sophisticated with their data. For example, Jet Blue's three scorecard categories of People, Performance, and Prosperity work well for the airline now, but it is a young and growing company. The metrics and architecture are likely to change as the company grows and matures. Don't get locked into some software that does not allow flexibility.

Requirement #3: Identification of Level, Trend, Analysis, and Action Plan

In addition to providing an overall view of the entire scorecard on one screen, users should be able to click on any individual analytic or metric and get answers to the four questions that should be asked about each performance measure:

1. **Level:** How are we doing right now compared to our target or historical data?
2. **Trend:** What is the trend in performance over time?
3. **Analysis:** Why are we seeing this level and trend in performance? What is causing it?
4. **Action Plan:** What are we doing to improve performance or keep it at its current good level?

Many scorecard software packages allow you to answer these four questions, but it takes many keystrokes and screens to get to and correlate the answers. Ideally, all four answers should be grouped in quadrants on one page so that users can see at a glance the information they need.

The next chapter describes how to develop customer analytics that provide a more accurate assessment of customer satisfaction and loyalty. These new analytics have been shown to measure customers' opinions and buying behavior accurately, and they are based on some of the best practices used in leading companies and government organizations.

4

Customer Relationship Analytics: Meaningful Metrics That Predict Loyalty

Now that you understand how to create an analytic, it is time to design some that are on the "Customer" section of your scorecard. This is one area where most organizations need a total overhaul of their existing metrics, which is a good reason to devote a chapter to this measure.

Customers are individuals who buy and use your products and services and mostly pay for them directly. Sometimes customers pay indirectly—for example, a patient in a hospital or a recipient of government services who pays via taxes. The purpose of the customer section of the scorecard is to tell managers whether or not the organization is doing a good job of meeting customer needs and whether or not it is going after appropriate new customers.

Most organizations have had customer measures on their scorecards for years, but most measures are fairly unsophisticated and yield little useful data. Annual surveys and complaints are still the predominant methods employed, and most customers do not complain or fill out surveys. Analytics are therefore well suited to measures of customer satisfaction, which is a complex dimension of performance that cannot be assessed with a single statistic or a one-question survey.

This chapter describes the goal of customer analytics; provides background on customer relationship management (CRM) and the flaws inherent in most CRM programs; and then describes in detail the four metrics needed to make a CRM program work: input metrics, process metrics, output metrics, and outcome metrics for managing customer relationships. The chapter also includes examples from clients who have developed innovative metrics and used them successfully—including an "aggravation" index, an "attractiveness" index, and an "ugly" stick to identify problem customers. But before we get to those solutions, let's make sure we understand the problem and the goal of customer analytics. Figure 4-1 lists the questions that should be answered by customer analytics.

The customer analytics section of the scorecard should provide answers to the following questions:

☐ Are we building strong relationships with the right customers to grow the business?

☐ Are we consistently meeting or exceeding customer expectations and making it easy to do business with our firm?

☐ Are we going after the right types of new business?

Figure 4-1. Questions Answered by Customer Analytics

Customer Metrics

The hierarchy of metrics in a typical customer section of a scorecard might look like the one shown in Figure 4-2.

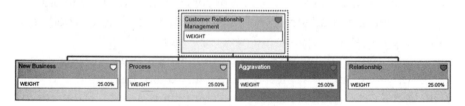

Figure 4-2. Customer Relationship Management Analytic

There are generally four types of measures that go into this section of a scorecard:

- Customer opinions, perceptions, and ratings
- Customer buying behavior
- Measures of internal processes to acquire customers and build relationships with them

- Measures of operational factors linked to important customer requirements.

Measuring the Relationships You Have With Customers

What this section of the scorecard is supposed to tell people is how good of a job we are doing at finding new customers, getting their business, and building strong and long-lasting profitable relationships with them. Even organizations that have a captive audience of customers need to worry about and measure how they do at customer relationship management. It seems so incredibly simple, yet it is done so poorly most of the time.

A personal example can easily illustrate this concept. I recently tried contacting my cell phone company to discuss a problem I was having with the service. I telephoned several times and gave up after a number of unsuccessful attempts and being put on hold for 30 minutes during each call. Then, I tried the company's friendly website, but there was no answer to my problem in the website's FAQ section. As a last resort, I decided to send the company an e-mail to see if my problem could be resolved. The next day I got an e-mail reply saying, "Thanks for your e-mail to customer service. We will get back to you with an answer within 7 days"! Now that's how to keep a customer happy.

This is not an unusual pattern for cell phone companies. In fact, the only thing that keeps most consumers from switching cell phone carriers is that they are locked into a contract; most customers learn from experience that they are all bad and that there are few, if any, options. Unfortunately, many other businesses are guilty of treating their customers in a similar fashion. These businesses would be wise to spend a lot less money on marketing and advertising for new customers and a lot more on taking care of the customers they already have. Sooner or later, a competitor will cash in on their woeful lack of attention to this matter.

Customer Relationship Management: Background

Customer relationship management, or CRM, is yet another one of those popular three-letter programs that have been implemented by most large corporations over the last decade and have failed to live up to expectations. CRM consultants sell software and processes that are supposed to make all of your customers love you and buy more of your stuff. But according to a study done by consulting firm Bearing Point in 2003, nearly half of the companies surveyed reported that they were reevaluating their CRM initiatives because of poor ROI. The study of 167 companies with at least $1 billion in sales indicated that although 82 percent felt that CRM was important, only 37 percent felt as if they were achieving expected performance. It is not surprising, therefore, that many of the organizations using CRM have no hard data on whether or not their CRM efforts have been successful. This is a serious problem. Any effort that costs as much to implement as CRM and takes up as much time needs to be measured and evaluated.

What CRM Is Supposed to Do and What It's *Not* Intended to Do

Most CRM programs consist of two parts:

- Processes for building relationships with customers that spell out behaviors and sequences for those activities.
- Software for creating customer databases and reporting progress in the sales/relationship building process with each account.

The theory behind CRM is that if companies take a systematic approach to building relationships with important customers, this will result in greater levels of customer satisfaction, increased revenue from those customers, and greater loyalty. This is a valid theory, but many CRM programs I have seen are thinly disguised attempts to cross-sell customers more of what they don't really need. CRM, in other words, has become a different way of asking, "Would you like fries with that?"

Another personal example shows exactly how this works. My banker wants to have a quarterly meeting with me so we can "review my holdings and my portfolio performance." I have no need to drive for 20 minutes to meet with him to review my accounts, which I can review online any time I want. What my banker really wants to do is get me into his office so he can talk me into putting more money in my accounts or to sell me additional products/services. He has sales goals he needs to achieve, and this is an easy way to achieve them. Because I have several different accounts at this bank, my banker has access to information he can use to his advantage, to tailor his sales pitch to my personal situation. He might, for example, say, "I noticed you have a lot of money in your checking account and thought you might want to put some of that into a CD to get a better interest rate." But building a relationship with a customer is more than just selling that customer more stuff. In fact, if the customer realizes he has been sold something he does not need, this tactic can jeopardize an otherwise healthy relationship.

CRM Is Based on Faulty Assumptions

There are several flaws in the logic behind most CRM programs I have seen. The three described below are the most common.

Faulty assumption #1: Building a relationship requires a systematic process and management system. Anyone who has ever had a job in sales knows that you can't take the same approach to sales as you take with engineering a product or landing a plane. You can follow the exact same series of behaviors with two different prospects, but one prospect may buy nothing and another may buy quite a bit of what you are selling. All customers want many of the same things when they buy something: value, convenience, the right features, and quality—and they want to buy from someone they can trust. Beyond that, there are many differences that influence people's buying behavior. The flawed logic in CRM programs is that it presumes you can engineer a relationship with the customer with as much precision as you can design the products or services you sell. This is simply not the case.

Selling is about 40 percent science, and 60 percent art. Yet many CRM programs focus on following the same series of behaviors with each customer. The most successful salespeople are those who can tailor their approach to each individual customer, which means getting to know them and doing more listening than talking. Using an engineering approach to sales tends to work well only with products that pretty much sell themselves, like fast food or cars.

Lisa, a friend who works as a pharmaceutical sales rep spends her days visiting doctors, trying to engage them in conversations, and leaving them samples. Each evening she needs to input data in the company's CRM system detailing which doctors she visited, how much time she spent with each doctor, what was said, how they responded, etc. Her job is not selling drugs to doctors' offices. Her job is to *build a relationship* with doctors so that they prescribe her company's drugs more often.

The problem with this approach is that the doctors are often too busy to spend any time with Lisa and she frequently spends most of her time trying to talk the office staff into letting her spend a minute or two with the doctor. She always manages to give away the free samples, but regularly leaves without getting to see the doctor. Realizing that doctors are busy during the day, her employer gives her a generous allowance to take doctors out to dinner after work, but Lisa never manages to spend her entertainment budget because most of the doctors want to be home with their families. Those who do want to go out to dinner are the single ones who want to date her. The company's attempts to boil down customer relationships to measures of call frequency, call duration, and following a scripted sales pitch simply do not work very well.

Bill, another friend, seems to do everything that would make a CRM consultant cringe. His behavior would lead you to believe that no one would ever buy anything from him—ever—but he is the most successful of all the consultants in the large firm for which he works. He starts a project with a new client and, within a year, has turned that client's business into a key account, generating many billable days for him and other consultants, and millions in sales of training materials.

What's his secret? He smokes, swears, frequently pisses off important people in the client organization, beats his client at pool, and is brutally honest with everyone. He does not report in to his boss, misses sales meetings, and is generally regarded in his firm as someone who is "not a team player." In spite of all this, his clients love him, trust him, and listen to his advice. In other words, Bill builds relationships with his clients. He is honest and trustworthy, and his clients see these qualities beneath his very brash exterior. Clients also like him because he does not try to be likeable—he is a real person, not a $1,000 suit with a good haircut, an Ivy-league degree, and a mouthful of management buzz words.

Faulty assumption #2: CRM software provides the data needed to improve your ability to build relationships with customers. Most CRM databases I have seen include all sorts of information about accounts and individual customers. They are filled with information about the organizational structure and who has the real authority, decision-making matrices, and personal information about customers, such as their previous jobs, buying history, spouses' names, kids' ages and names, hobbies, interests, golf scores, favorite vacation spots, etc. Salespeople can access all of this data from their laptops; they can go from appointment to appointment and make each customer feel special by "remembering" all sorts of warm and fuzzy personal information about him or her.

The flaw in this logic is the erroneous belief that having this kind of customer intelligence will enable the salesperson to build a relationship with the customer. This logic brings to mind a movie called *Groundhog Day*, which featured a character played by Bill Murray. Murray's character has a love interest, played by Andie McDowell. To try to make her fall in love with him, he learns more and more about her each day, hoping to use this knowledge to his advantage. He discovers that she loves French poetry, hates white chocolate, always drinks to world peace, etc., and his strategy of using this information to woo her slowly starts to pay off. The woman eventually figures out she's being worked, and the scheme backfires. Only when Murray's character stops trying to trick her into loving him does she begin to grow fond of him.

The approach used by the film character is exactly the same as that used by many CRM programs: finding out detailed information about customers and recalling and using that information to try to build their trust. Almost invariably, a customer will get wise to this. Most customers eventually figure out that they are being worked, and none respond well to this tactic. The bottom line is that having a mass of personal information about a customer does not really help you build a relationship. In fact, it might alienate a customer who was just beginning to trust you, just as it backfired in *Groundhog Day*.

Faulty assumption #3: It will be easy for salespeople to use the CRM software, and they will love it when they see how it helps them sell more. I have a lot of friends and clients in sales jobs in pharmaceuticals, insurance, financial services, medical devices, copiers, and a host of other products and services. One thing they all agree about is that they hate their companies' stupid CRM systems. They particularly hate spending 2 to 4 hours a day with their laptops, typing in reports of conversations with customers and prospects, entering data, and preparing account status reports. Most have a large territory to cover, so they spend from 7:00 A.M. until 6:00 P.M. on the road, visiting customers. The CRM data has to be entered each night, after the salespeople are stressed out all day from traffic and customers who didn't want to see them. They universally despise the CRM system and see the system requirements as busywork that detracts from their productivity and negatively affects their morale.

The CRM systems I have seen are neither simple nor intuitive, and they require a lot of time from salespeople. Of course, if all of this time spent entering and retrieving information paid off, it might be worth it, but most studies I have seen suggest that CRM does not produce good ROI. What is not discussed in any of these studies is the impact these systems have on the *morale* of the sales force. Anecdotal data reveals that CRM systems contribute to stress and poor morale among salespeople. The only people who seem to like CRM systems are managers who feel comfortable with the enormous volume of data they can store and generate. Managers like to keep tabs on their people and make sure they are not goofing off; daily CRM reports like those described above ensure that the salespeople are out there every day calling on prospects and servicing their existing accounts. Unfortunately, this frequently does not produce increased sales or loyalty from customers.

How to Measure CRM

If your organization uses CRM and avoids the faulty assumptions presented above, the system does have some advantages, but only if it is measured and monitored. As with any aspect of performance or improvement program, it is unlikely that you will be able to come up with a single metric that tells you whether or not you are successful. No single chart will tell you this. Instead, what is needed is a *customer relationship analytic* that comprises four types of metrics:

- **Input metrics**—measures of quality, accuracy, thoroughness, and the degree to which data are current and verifiable; these may also include measures of leads, prospects, proposals, or bids for new business.
- **Process metrics**—measures of behavior or activity proven to link to good performance and better relationships with customers
- **Output metrics**—quantifiable things that can be counted, such as orders, samples distributed, proposals submitted, new clients acquired, brochures sent, phone calls made, meetings held, accounts visited, demos conducted, etc.
- **Outcome metrics**—gross margin dollars, sales revenue, reduced marketing costs, partnerships with important customers.

When creating a CRM Analytic, begin by assigning a weight to each of the four types of measures, as shown in Figure 4-3.

Figure 4-3. Sample Weight of Each of the 4 Customer Relationship Analytics

The reason for such a heavy weight on the outputs and outcomes is that they are the real measures of value. In fact, if you asked any company why it is doing CRM, the answer would match the things listed under "outcome metrics"because these are the only things that put dollars into a bank account. The problem with outcome and even some output metrics, however, is that they are mostly *lagging indicators* or measures of the *past*. And, as previously mentioned, a good CRM Index or Analytic should include *a mix of leading and lagging indicators* in order to be a valid gauge. The leading indicators are the ones that track the inputs and the process or behavior measures. Tracking these metrics on a daily basis helps sales managers feel secure that their people are out there working hard. Let's look at each measure in more detail.

Input Metrics for Measuring Customer Relationships

Input measures are important because they are the most forward-looking of all the four types of measures in the CRM Index. Input measures should be both quantitative and qualitative. Some examples of input metrics that might be counted are:

- Inquiries received
- Website hits
- Calls made
- Letters sent
- Customer profiles created

- Attendees at seminars
- Business cards received
- Brochures sent
- Leads generated
- RFPs received

These are all measures of activities designed to generate new business or gain additional business from existing customers. But simply counting things like those listed above is not enough. The input metrics need to have a *qualitative* component as well.

Measure the *Quality* of Your Inputs

About 70 people from 25 different companies attended a public workshop I conducted last year at a conference in Orlando, Florida. The input metrics that I tracked looked very strong: About 30 of the attendees gave me their business cards and asked for mine after the session. I followed up several times with letters, phone calls, books, etc.—but not one of those prospects generated a dollar in income for me. Quantitatively, the metrics were fine; qualitatively, however, something was obviously not so fine.

Not long after this, one of my clients who is in the police radio business came up with a qualitative measure of prospects called "Opportunity Strategic Value," or OSV Score. He assigned each prospect a score from 0–100 percent, depending on factors such as:

- Location
- Size
- Name recognition (i.e., companies that would impress other police departments if he had them as customers)
- Number of units needed
- Potential gross margin
- Political connections (e.g., does he have any friends working there)

Account managers were measured on the inputs they generated, but also on the *quality* of those inputs. This helped drive the right behavior by getting them to focus on bringing in important and *profitable* customers.

Another client in the facilities maintenance business came up with a similar metric for both prospective and existing customers, and he had similar success with using the measure to encourage salespeople to go after high-quality prospective customers. Points were also assessed for different types of inputs, such as 10 points for a business card or letter sent, to 75 points for an RFP received.

Each of these examples points out one important fact. If you hope to succeed with CRM, it is important to measure the *quality* of your input as well as the quantity.

Process Metrics for Measuring Customer Relationships

Process measures in sales or account management are usually measures of *behavior* or *activity*. For example, a process metric might be the number of accounts called on per week, or the number of product demonstrations conducted, or the number of customers who attended your golf outing. Many organizations have very specific standards for following processes that are supposed to build relationships with customers, for example, visiting A-level customers once a week, B-level customers once a month, and so forth. Frequently, there are also standards for how to give a presentation or demonstration, right down to the exact words to say and the precise hand movements to use to demonstrate a product. Salespeople are measured on the degree to which their behavior matches the standards. Call centers that deal with customers also have process measures, which include call waiting time, abandoned calls (i.e., hang-ups), average call length, and so on.

All of these process measures and standards are designed to increase sales, improve customer satisfaction, and increase customer loyalty. The problem with most of these process measures is that in most companies, they have not been *proven* to link to anything of value. In other words, there is no evidence suggesting that following a scripted demo or visiting accounts once a week results in increased business or even increased customer satisfaction. This differs markedly from the results from other metrics—most companies, for example, usually have fairly good data on the link between input metrics and output metrics. A good illustration of this comes from a friend who sells executive compensation plans. He sends out about 100 letters to get 15 good leads that he calls to get 5 appointments to do 3 proposals to get 1 sale. With data like this, it is fairly easy to set targets for input metrics, based on overall sales goals.

However, I rarely see this kind of research backing up the validity of process measures. The process measures and standards are too frequently based on anecdotal evidence or superstition. Sales managers feel good if all their reps are calling on the right number of accounts, conducting demonstrations, handing out business cards, and entering all these activities on a daily basis into the CRM database. Often, the people who get the best scores on the process or behavior measures are among the worst performers and achieve little of value. In contrast, there are people like my friend Bill who ignore the CRM protocol on behavior or process measures, do not dress appropriately, refrain from using company lingo when describing products or services, cancel client dinners at the last minute or refuse to socialize with clients at all, and do not work well with other company consultants and salespeople. In spite of this, their performance on the *outcome* measures beats that of their peers, and their achievements are substantially better.

The key to having good process metrics in your CRM Index is to study the behavior of your superstar salespeople or customer contact employees closely. Do not interview them—*watch* them. Most people who are good at what they do are unconsciously competent, and they have a hard time articulating why they are successful. By watching the star performers and comparing their behavior to the average, you are likely to find subtle differences that account for their success. These are the subtle differences upon which your process metrics should be based. By deriving your process measures from a study of your star performers, you create a pretty good hypothesis about how following a particular process or sequence of behavior can improve performance.

Test such hypotheses, however, before settling on them and making them a template for the way you do business. Also, keep in mind that there is a lot of art to managing customer relationships, and the more you try to adopt a cookie-cutter approach, the less likely your salespeople are to be successful. Follow an approach used and recommended by Nordstrom: Hire people with brains and personalities, and trust them to make good judgments rather than turning them into robots.

Even though there is a lot of art to sales or relationship building, some basic processes should be followed and measured. For example, there may be a process for interviewing a prospect and defining his or her needs. There may be another process for determining and overcoming objections, and another process for reviewing the strengths of your product or service and comparing them to your competition's product or service.

Extraordinarily simple processes are sometimes extraordinarily effective. Baptist Hospital in Pensacola, Florida, a winner of the prestigious Malcolm Baldrige Award, found that asking patients a single question each day dramatically improved patient satisfaction. Hospital supervisors made it a standard for all nurses, aides, and patient contact employees; the simple process and the almost absurdly simple question reaped great results. The question, by the way, was "Is there anything else I can do to make you more comfortable today?"

Note, however, that a standardized script or a strictly defined process is not the best approach in all cases. Each approach needs to be custom tailored to a particular situation or individual customer.

Behavior is sometimes difficult to quantify, and the reason process metrics are given such a low weight in the CRM Index is that behavior or process metrics are the measures with the *least integrity*. In other words, an organization can be getting a good score on all the behavior measures and still have unhappy customers and problems with relationships. Input metrics are a little less risky because they involve tracking hard objective things like leads or requests for quotations/proposals.

However, if you back your behavior and process metrics with solid research, you might want to try increasing the weight of these measures in the CRM Index to make them equal to the input metrics. In this case, the input and process metrics would each be worth 12.5 percent of the index.

Output Metrics for Measuring Customer Relationships

An output is some sort of product or something that can be counted—i.e., either a physical product (such as a proposal, report, or contract) or an accomplishment (such as a closed deal, a new client brought on board, an order, or a service performed successfully). A specific output measure for a shipping firm might be packages or containers delivered; for an airline, it might be on-time flights. Outputs tend to be things of value, either to the organization or to its customers. Customer contact employees—such as account managers, service delivery personnel, and customer service reps—generate all sorts of outputs that might be counted as part of a CRM Analytic.

In a previous chapter, I mentioned that a number of my clients have a metric called "the Aggravation Index," which tracks the number of things they do each day that aggravate their customers. Each aggravation is also weighted on a 1 to 10 scale, based on the severity of its damage potential. The index is a remarkably good indicator of what makes customers unhappy enough to leave. In other words, there is a direct correlation between the aggravation index, which is an *output* metric, and customer loyalty, which is an *outcome* measure. In general, the aggravations are not caused by the salesperson or account rep but by the people involved in delivering the service to the customer. One illustration of this comes from an airline's aggravation index, which counts the following factors:

- Late flights
- Cancelled flights
- Delays taking off

- Dropped calls
- Hard to use website
- Customer complaints

- Delays waiting for bags
- Lost bags
- Damaged bags
- Long hold time when calling to reserve a ticket

- Middle seats
- Long lines to get boarding passes
- Gates without enough chairs

Each of these aggravations is counted on a daily basis and multiplied by the number of passengers impacted and by the seriousness of the aggravation. For example, a flight that is 30 minutes late would count a lot less than one that is cancelled, causing 200 passengers to spend the night in O'Hare because every hotel room in Chicago is booked.

StoraEnso, the oldest corporation in the world, is in the paper and forest products business. It has developed a Customer Aggravation Analytic that includes the factors shown in Figure 4-4, each weighted differently based on the degree to which it aggravates a customer:

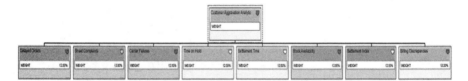

Figure 4-4. Sample Customer Aggravation Analytic for a Paper Company

The key thing for this or any other Customer Aggravation Analytic you might construct is that the data is not gathered via a survey. Instead, the factors that aggravate a customer are identified via focus groups, and it is these focus groups that rate and rank the severity of the aggravations. Once you have this data, you count the number of times each aggravating event occurs and multiply the frequency by the severity weight. StoraEnso takes this one step further by assigning a weight to the customer, based on the size and importance of that customer's business. Obviously, making a really big customer really upset can be devastating. StoraEnso has found that there is a high correlation between keeping aggravations to a minimum and maintaining customer loyalty, which has clear links to profitability, so this is a metric that executives monitor very carefully.

How your company performs or how your products perform has a major impact on the relationship with your customers. If the copy machines in your law firm break down too frequently, it can ruin your efforts to build a relationship with a customer. The copy machine account rep and repair technician are the ones who should take the heat for this, but the customer sees a problem with your organization. It is wise to remember that how a customer feels about your firm is determined mostly by your product and service—not by the pleasant salesperson or account rep.

When tracking outputs, therefore, it is important to include those produced by the salespeople or customer contact people and those that reflect how customers perceive product and service. Most of the things that cause a relationship between two companies to sour are not the fault of salespeople or account reps. The most important outputs relate to *how well products and services perform*. Outputs are given a fairly heavy weight in the CRM Analytic for two reasons:

- They can be objectively counted and measured, and
- They have a big impact on the relationship with customers.

Other outputs for the sales or account management function can also be included in the CRM Analytic. In fact, there may be a long list of outputs that get counted and assigned a weight, depending on their importance to the organization's success. For example, a proposal for a $1million sale might be worth less than a signed contract for $200,000. Some of the outputs you may want to incorporate into your outcomes metrics list follow:

- Proposals won
- New customers acquired
- Extensions or sales of additional items
- Referrals
- Commendation letters from customers
- Awards from customers
- Joint marketing efforts with customers
- Customer problems solved

When constructing this section of your CRM Analytic, think about assigning a weight to the various outputs based on how important they are to the relationship you have with your customers. With this in mind, you will probably benefit from counting the outputs that relate to your product or service performing well as worth 25 percent of the total 35 percent, and the remaining 10 percent for the outputs produced by the salespeople or account reps. Although a big sale is an important output for the company and the salesperson, it does not necessarily strengthen the relationship a customer has with your company.

Outcome Metrics for Measuring Customer Relationships

Outputs are products or accomplishments that can be easily counted or quantified. An output might have obvious value (such as an order) or hopefully lead to something of value (such as a proposal submitted). *Outcomes*, on the other hand, tend to be things that are harder to quantify and measure, but they are often more important than the outputs. For example, a long-term trusting relationship with a profitable customer is an important outcome that is harder to measure than the number of responses to a direct mail marketing campaign.

Remember that the goal of a CRM process is to build a strong, positive, and lasting relationship with important customers that lead to greater profits. A number of client firms have designed a Customer Relationship Analytic that is used as a measure of the type of relationship they have with each account. Among these is a facilities service firm in San Jose, which calls this metric "the Customer Relationship Index." A textile firm in Orange County, California, has a similar metric, which it has cleverly named its "Matrimonial Index."

In each of these companies, the metrics scale starts at a level-1 relationship, which indicates that the customer is 'married' to another supplier but willing to have a friendly lunch or take an occasional phone call from their sales reps. A level-5 relationship indicates a happy customer who has been buying from the company for several years, and has gotten to know the account rep and others in the company very well.

A score of 10 on the relationship index is used to signify a true 'marriage' or business partnership. A 10 score might indicate a long-term contract, many personal friendships among the employees of the organization and the customer, political connections (e.g., the company CEO and the customer's CEO are personal friends), exit barriers that would make it difficult and expensive for the customer to find a new supplier, etc.

Both firms have specific criteria for each number of the 'matrimonial' index that are measures of the strength of the relationship. Another client incorporates an input measure that the CEO calls the "ugly stick," with the outcome metric called the relationship index. There are two dimensions that go into calculating this index:

- Attractiveness   1–10 scale
- Relationship   1–10 scale.

A "perfect 10" or "attractive" customer is one who has the following characteristics:

- Pays invoices in 30 days or less;
- Generates healthy profit margins;
- Buys large volumes;
- Partners with suppliers;
- Is a stable company that will be around a long time;
- Is an ethical company that manages with integrity;
- Has a customer name that will impress other potential customers; and
- Is easy to work with (e.g., low maintenance).

A level-1 or "ugly" customer would be just the opposite. Customer accounts are given an "ugly stick" rating twice a year by those who work with them because their status often changes over time. Some customers get uglier with time, and some get better looking. For example, a successful major airline might have been rated as a 9 in attractiveness several years ago, but it has fallen to a level-2 now because it is close to filing for bankruptcy.

The 1 to 10 relationship index is also an important outcome measure. The company sets targets for certain types of customers and for the types of relationship it wants to have with them. An example of how one company constructs this metric is shown in Figure 4-5.

Attractiveness Level	Relationship Target
Beautiful 9–10	9–10 happy marriage/partnership
Very attractive 7–8	7–8 engaged; happy relationship
Attractive, but some flaws 5–6	5–6 committed dating, mostly good relationship
Average, a number of flaws 3–4	3–4 casual dating, no real trust yet; customer using other suppliers
Ugly, many flaws 1–2	1–2 occasional lunch, customer "married" to another supplier.

Figure 4-5. Sample Customer Attractiveness/Relationship Index

The relationship index should probably be one of the heavily weighted sub-measures in the outcome segment of your CRM Index. Other important outcomes should probably be included as well:

- $ in sales increases from existing customers
- $ in gross margin increases from existing customers
- $ in new sales attributable to referrals from existing customers
- Customer satisfaction levels
- Accounts where your company is the sole supplier
- Accounts where your company is rated as a preferred supplier

Conclusions

Most organizations offer a product or service that can be bought elsewhere. Customers have more choices today than ever before about where to spend their money and where to send their business. In response to this, many organizations—from government to education to healthcare—are measuring customer satisfaction and trying to improve it. Yet, the metrics used to assess customer satisfaction are no better today than they were 20 years ago. In some cases, the measures have gotten worse. *A 1-question survey that asks about your willingness to recommend is no better than a 10-question survey—it is still just a survey!* Moreover, there is no guarantee that it will be filled out.

Recognizing this, leading organizations are coming up with better and more innovative measures of customer satisfaction and the relationships they have with customers. Even organizations with a captive audience of customers need to measure customer satisfaction. If you do a bad enough job, customers will eventually look elsewhere for the product or service you provide. Therefore, the customer analytics section of your scorecard should provide answers to the following questions:

- Are we pursuing the right types of new business?
- Do we employ an effective systematic process for building strong relationships with customers?
- Do we make it easy and hassle-free for customers to do business with our organization?
- Do our products/services consistently meet or exceed customer expectations and requirements?
- Have we built strong relationships with important customers to ensure their future loyalty and recommendations?

Organizations have been conducting CRM for decades—it is not something new. Sales have always been about building relationships, and there have been many successful salespeople over the years, even without flowcharts on the selling process or CRM software and a laptop computer. Over the years, however, some companies have invested millions of dollars in software, training, and meetings, hoping to standardize or improve their relationships with customers. What many of these companies have *not* done is to measure the *effectiveness* of their CRM efforts. A single measure of something as complex as customer relationships is unlikely to reflect performance. What is needed is a Customer Relationship Analytic that summarizes results for four different aspects of performance:

- Inputs
- Processes or behaviors
- Outputs
- Outcomes

Such an index, which is focused and specific, can provide executives with the data they need to monitor their company's progress in creating and sustaining positive and profitable relationships with important customers.

The next chapter describes how to develop external analytics. External metrics are best represented as analytics because there are a wide range of external factors that can have a major impact on most organizations. Measures for these factors, vital for predicting success and determining strategies, are rarely included in organizational scorecards, an omission that is almost incomprehensible.

Key Points to Keep in Mind
About Customer Metrics and Analytics

☐ Most scorecards today do include measures of customer satisfaction and loyalty.

☐ Most metrics in this area are seriously flawed. They produce data that lacks integrity, captures only a small sample of customers, and does not link to future buying behavior.

☐ Organizations need to be careful to attract the right new customers and should have a metric that reveals more than just sales growth—they need to look at the quality of those new accounts/customers.

☐ Customers tend to look for a new supplier after multiple bad experiences and aggravations, and the vast majority do not fill out a survey or complain—they just walk.

☐ Organizations need to have a metric that tells them how many things they screw up on a daily basis, and how bad those screw-ups are, so they can gauge the level of customer frustration and aggravation.

☐ Building relationships with customers is more of an art than a science, so process measures should focus on proven behaviors that strengthen relationships rather than logic and things that are easy to count.

☐ Most scorecards need to have an outcome metric that provides data on the health of the relationships a company has with various customers. The goal is to have the right level of partnership with the right customers to drive profitability and success.

5

External Analytics: Quantifying Factors That Can Make or Break Your Business

The purpose of the metrics described in this chapter is to quantify external factors and variables that could have a huge impact on your organization's performance. Like any metric, External Analytics should consist of factors that can be measured on a regular basis rather than as single events. A pilot, for example, monitors many metrics relating to weather, such as wind speeds, rain/snow, and cloud cover. A hurricane like Katrina is also an external factor that would have an obvious impact on the pilot, but it is an *event*, not a metric.

External metrics have the same characteristics as other types of metrics on an organization's scorecard, except that the organization has little or no control or influence over many of these measures. Interest rates have a huge impact on revenue and profits for a mortgage company, but there is not much the company can do to influence those rates. Similarly, the cost of energy is a big line item for many manufacturing and processing companies, but not much can be done about that either.

These and similar external factors can have a huge impact on most if not all of the other measures on a company's scorecard. Therefore, not attempting to quantify these factors and watch them on a regular basis would be a huge mistake, and this applies to all organizations—corporate, government, and nonprofit. The scorecard of a government organization needs to monitor things like brand image on a regular basis, just as Pepsi or Nike would. Defense companies need to monitor threats and defense spending on a regular basis, as changes can have a big positive or negative impact on their business. Being shut down by a regulatory agency or losing an important partner or supplier can also be a shock; if you see it coming, you can prepare for it. External metrics need not always be warnings of impending doom; they might show something very positive. Over the last few years, for example, the demand for housing has been a positive gauge for homebuilders.

Figure 5-1 lists the questions that should be answered by External Analytics, and Figure 5-2 lists the types of external metrics that you should measure. These are discussed in detail later in this chapter.

External Analytics should answer the following questions for an organization:

- [ ] How well known are we, and what is our brand image?
- [ ] What is going on in the world (politics, economics, etc.) that could impact our organization?
- [ ] At what level of risk is our organization from competitive and other types of threats?
- [ ] What type of relationships do we have with our key suppliers and partners?
- [ ] How are we doing at meeting regulatory and legal requirements?

Figure 5-1. Questions Answered by External Analytics

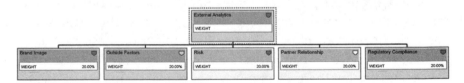

Figure 5-2. Types of External Metrics

Brand Image: Measuring It in Your Organization

Big corporations spend millions to make people aware of their companies and their products and services and to think good things about them. Just think for a moment about how Pepsi and Coca-Cola try to outdo each other with better and better commercials. The logos of both companies are recognized in every country of the world. Brand image is just as important in government and nonprofit organizations.

In many cases, however, increased awareness about these organizations is evidence of something that has gone wrong. One illustration of this is the heightened awareness about FEMA in the last few years. Media attention, mostly negative, has made almost everyone in the United States learn what FEMA is and what it does (or doesn't do). The same can be said about Enron, which has earned a brand image for itself that no organization wants.

Creating a Brand Metric

There are two general dimensions that go into a brand metric for a business: awareness and image. In other words, how many people know who you are (i.e., your company or organization) and what you do? What do they think of you? For government organizations, image is usually much more important than awareness. Government organizations spend a tremendous amount of money on "outreach" (the government's term for what the corporate world calls "marketing") to make their image more attractive to citizens of this country and to the world beyond U.S. borders.

Awareness data is typically gathered by telephone or mail surveys; occasionally this data gathering is conducted in person, at malls or at big events attended by many people. Typically, the surveyor asks each respondent to list three major discount airlines, or hotel chains, or computer brands, or whatever reflects the industry you are in, and tracks how many respondents list your company name without being prompted. If you have any doubt about how much awareness data matters, just ask a group of people to list three soft drinks. You can bet that Pepsi and Coke make the list 100 percent of the time.

Measuring brand awareness for a government organization is a little more complicated. Government organizations are not interested in how many people know their names or logos; they are more interested if taxpayers or customers know what they do. Such organizations often discover that people are confused or totally in the dark about their purpose and/or function. When managers of the Santa Clara Valley Water District in San Jose, California, asked local residents what they thought the water district does, they found that most people thought the district supplied them with the water coming from their faucets. This was only indirectly true. The SCVWD is a wholesaler of water that sells water to cities, which, in turn, sell the water to consumers and businesses.

The second question that concerns organizations is "What do people think of us and our products or services?" Collecting data that answers this question can be somewhat complicated. Figure 5-3 lists some of the sources clients have used in gathering data that can be productively used in a brand analytic.

☐ Newspaper/press clippings

☐ Survey/interview/focus group data

☐ Internet blogs

☐ Website hits or Google/Yahoo searches

☐ Broker ratings

☐ Stock price

☐ Letters to the editor in magazines and newspapers

☐ Awards and recognition received by the organization

☐ Resumes received from potential employees

☐ Rankings and ratings by magazines and professional associations

☐ Number of people who see your advertising/marketing and the number of times they see it

☐ Attendance at company-sponsored events or community meetings

☐ Support/endorsement by influential people such as politicians and industry big shots

☐ Data from exit interviews from employees who quit

Figure 5-3. Checklist of Possible Sources for
Gathering Data for a Brand Analytic

There are a number of other metrics that could go into a brand metric (such as brand loyalty of customers or repeat business), but these are better measures for the customer section of your scorecard (refer back to Chapter 4 for details). The focus of the brand metric is people's opinions, not their buying behavior. The brand analytic is a leading indicator for an organization and should not include any out-come measures. (The only exception to this may be stock price.)

The difficult part of creating a brand metric is figuring out how to *quantify* the information sources listed above. In quantifying any of the data above, you need to consider four factors:

1. *How many people were exposed to the information about our organization?* An article in the *Washington Post* counts a lot more than a community meeting attended by only 30 people.
2. *How much information were they exposed to that could influence their perception or opinion of your company or organization in a positive or negative way?* A 50-word article in the back of a small hometown newspaper does not count the same as a 20-minute segment on *Dateline*.
3. *What is the credibility and level of influence of the source of the information?* A story in a tabloid might not have as much credibility as one in the *New York Times*.
4. *To what degree was the information positive or negative?* Your own marketing or advertising would probably be close to 100 percent positive, whereas the press loves to print bad news, so it would probably be rare to have a segment on the evening news about how great your company's products or services are. Bad news does increase brand awareness, but not necessarily brand image. Unless you are a Hollywood star, you want to avoid it.

Organizations that track a brand analytic or metric on their score-cards usually calculate their performance on a daily or weekly basis. You can make this as complicated or simple as your needs and resources dictate. My company (which is one guy working out of the house) has a fairly simple brand metric that consists of the following components:

- Website hits: 10 percent
- Book sales: 30 percent
- Attendees at my workshops and speeches: 50 percent
- Citations: 10 percent (I can track this for free, thanks to amazon.com)

I do get occasional press coverage (interviews, newspaper articles, etc.), but this is so infrequent that I don't need to quantify it in my metric.

A big corporation or government organization has many staff members to figure out how to track and calculate a more sophisticated brand analytic. Advertising agencies and marketing firms can also track the impact of specific ads and communication techniques. A brand analytic for a business might be designed like the one shown in Figure 5-4.

Brand Awareness 30%	Brand Image 70%		
	Opinions 40%	Ratings 20%	Marketing 40%
	Analysts 30%	Stock Price 30%	Trade/Press 40%
	Consumer 50%	Prof./Business 30%	Awards/Ratings 20%

Figure 5-4. Sample Brand Analytic

Outside Factors: Measuring Their Influence on Your Business

Outside factors are metrics of variables in the outside world that can have a huge impact on the success of your business. If you are in the real estate business, four factors have a big impact on your success: available inventory (i.e., houses for sale), interest rates, demand for housing in the area you serve, and housing prices. Any one of these variables can affect your business in a positive or negative way. There are other external factors that might be tracked for your real estate business, such as the local economy, consumer price index, employment, job growth, etc. However, it is important to limit the external factors that you measure to 2 to 6 metrics that are specifically related to your business and customer base and that directly impact your performance.

Creating an Outside Factors Analytic

A good place to start in creating this analytic is to list the reports and data that you currently review that have an impact on your business. Next, add a list of outside metrics that you don't currently review but might consider looking at in your analytic. Often, these are things that may be difficult to quantify, but they could be the most important factors to think about.

One external factor that might go on the dashboard of a medical devices company (such as Medtronic, which makes pacemakers and similar equipment) is the leanings of government (which affects Medicare) and health insurance companies toward paying for their products when patients need them. Politics are also an important external factor that might be considered for your analytic. Figure 5-5 lists the major types of external factors to think about when constructing your analytic.

☐ Economic trends in the industries/markets you serve
☐ Economic trends in your own industry/market
☐ Regulatory changes
☐ Politics
☐ Customer trends/preferences
☐ Research studies/new data

Figure 5-5. Major Types of External Events to Consider When Constructing an Outside Factors Analytic

Example #1: An Outside Factors Analytic for a Jet Maintenance Company

Figure 5-6 shows what an outside factors analytic might look like for a company that does maintenance on jets for big U.S. airlines.

External Factor #1: The Number of Jets in Service. Because this company provides service to the airlines, it is important for it to track the number of aircraft that are actively in service and the age of the fleet. After September 11, 2001, the airlines parked a number of jets out in the desert in storage because demand for air travel was way down. This means that there was less need for maintenance.

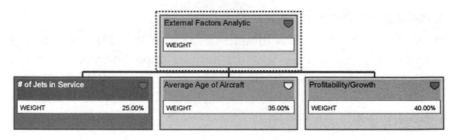

Figure 5-6. Sample Outside Factors Analytic for an Airline Maintenance Company

External Factor #2: The Age of the Jets. The average age for jets is measured in both years and flight miles. Southwest Airlines has a fairly new fleet of jets, but they are heavily used, so they might require more frequent maintenance and repair than a 777 fleet that is not actively used or not flying as many hours per week.

External Factor #3: Profitability and Growth. The profitability and growth of the airlines serviced by this company is also an important factor to measure in the analytic. In fact, it is given the highest weight in this example. Much of the work done by this maintenance company is discretionary or cosmetic, such as painting and maintaining the seats, tray tables, and passenger amenities. When airlines are financially strapped (as many have been in recent years), it is easy to defer minor maintenance items as long as they are not related to safety.

If your organization is an airline or a car company, the price of fuel might be a good metric to include in your outside factors analytic. If it is a fire department in California, the amount of rain would probably be a good factor to include on your scorecard, because low rain amounts increase the danger of brush fires.

Example #2: An Outside Factors Analytic for a Government Transportation Agency

Figure 5-7 shows what the outside factors analytic might look like for a state department of transportation (DOT) that builds and maintains roads, bridges, and highways.

Political factors are given the highest weight because politics impact spending for DOT projects. In California, that metric would

Population Changes	Political Factors	Fuel Prices	#/Type of Vehicles
30%	40%	10%	20%

Figure 5-7. Sample Outside Factors Analytic for a
State Department of Transportation

probably be green right now because Governor Schwarzenegger is planning to spend a lot of money in the next few years on more roads in the state, especially in areas where traffic is heaviest. Michigan's governor is also allocating money for repairing state roads and bridges, which have needed repair and resurfacing for years.

Population changes are an important factor to measure because more people mean more cars and trucks. Fuel prices have some impact on discretionary driving, but that is the lowest weighted factor. The final metric on the number and type of vehicles using state roads is also a factor, because heavy trucks and SUVs put more demand on roads than lighter passenger vehicles.

Of the four metrics in this outside factors analytic, three are very easy to measure and quantify. Political factors are the hardest to measure. The types of factors to track in a politics metric would include passage of bills/budgets, votes, new funding, elections, speech content, and campaign promises (although this last should probably be given a low weight).

Risk: Assessing Your Organization's Exposure

Risk is a very important metric for most types of organizations to include on their scorecards. It would never be possible to completely eliminate risk, but a good balanced scorecard should include an analytic that quantifies the level of risk an organization faces at any given time. This would allow for more intelligent decision making regarding the commitment of resources. Organizations expend a lot of resources trying to minimize various types of risks, but very few quantify their levels of risk or threat and put them on the executive scorecard.

A good example of a risk analytic in the government is the Homeland Security Advisory System risk metric. This metric ranges from a low risk of terrorist threat (green) to a severe threat (red). A number of individual factors must be considered when establishing this metric, so it is a good example of an analytic. One of the problems with this metric is that the general public does not understand what the ratings mean or how people should change their behavior in response to the ratings. Author Donald Fischer has created an excellent analytic for organizations to use in assessing their preparedness for security threats. Fisher's suggested analytic is depicted in Figure 5-8, which shows a scorecard that examines the level of threat (red to green) and the level of preparedness. Preparedness is assessed using three metrics derived from the Baldrige Award criteria: approach, deployment, and results.

Zero-Based Preparation   **World-Class Preparation**

| 0 | 10 | 20 | 30 | 40 | 50 | 60 | 70 | 80 | 90 | 100 |

| Green | Blue | Yellow | Orange | Red |
| (Low) | (Guarded) | (Elevated) | (High) | (Severe) |

(Circle Appropriate Percentile)

Figure 5-8. Security Threat Analytic

Creating a Risk Analytic

The major types of risks or threats that should be considered when developing a risk analytic are listed in Figure 5-9.

☐ Competitive threats
☐ Environmental risks or threats
☐ Safety and security threats
☐ Risks associated with research findings
☐ Legal risks
☐ Technology threats and risks

Figure 5-9. Major Risks and Threats to Consider When Constructing a Risk Analytic

When developing a risk analytic for your organization, the first step is to use the list presented above to identify the types of threats that could impact your organization in a big way. Next, establish weights based on the importance of each risk factor. The final step is to determine how to assess the level of risk for each factor. Remember that this metric is a *leading* indicator, not a measure of bad things that have already happened.

The types of risks that get addressed in this metric will vary considerably, depending on the nature of the organization. The risk analytic for a bank might look at security measures that prevent identity theft by cyber-criminals and direct theft of cash from bank branches. In contrast, the risk analytic for CalTrans or another state department of transportation might look at preparedness for weather emergencies like floods, hurricanes, or even major snowstorms.

Risk Management Solutions of Newark, California, is working on an interesting metric that would fall into this category. The company has already come up with a metric that helps predict what it calls "Nat-Cats"—natural catastrophes such as storms and earthquakes. Risk Management Solutions is also now teaming with Rand to come up with a metric that predicts "L-Cats"—liability catastrophes. Both of these metrics appear to be promising contenders for future scorecards even though the "L-Cats" analytic will not be ready for market until sometime in 2009. Regardless of which risk factor your organization chooses to address, you must establish clear measurement dimensions. The following questions can be used for this purpose:

- What is the probability or likelihood of a negative event? (0–100 percent)
- What is the impact of the event on our organization? (0–100, ranging from very minor to devastating)
- What is our level of preparedness? (0–100 percent prepared)

For this analytic to show good performance, you must define and meet the highest level of preparedness for the risks, the highest probability of occurrence, and the highest impact on the organization. You will never get to a point of zero risk, but the green zone should lie within an acceptable range of minimum risk and maximum preparedness.

Partnerships: Measuring Their Performance and Strength

Most organizations today are not self-sufficient entities and rely on a wide network of suppliers, vendors, and partners—outside organizations that help them succeed. Some government organizations use outside contractors to do most of their work: Savannah River, a Department of Energy facility in Aiken, South Carolina, which has only about 500 federal government employees but about 5,000 contractors working at the site is a typical example. Car companies rely on dealerships, which are independent businesses, to sell and repair the cars they manufacture. Air Products and Chemicals of Allentown, Pennsylvania, spends 66 cents of every dollar in operating expense on outside suppliers. All of these examples point to the importance of partnerships with outside organizations. Yet most organizational scorecards do not have a measure of the strength of these partnerships. At best, there is a measure of suppliers' performance on a couple of lagging indicators like on-time deliveries or accurate orders.

Creating a Partner Relationship Analytic

Two fairly broad questions can help you determine what needs to be measured in a partner relationship metric:

1. How important is this organization to our success?
2. How strong is the relationship between our two firms?

To answer the first question, you need to establish a 1 to 100 or 1 to 10 rating scale for each of your suppliers, based on the types of factors listed in Figure 5-10. Each supplier/partner should be rated by knowledgeable individuals in your organization at least 4 times a year so that any change in status is not missed.

The second part of this analytic is a rating of 1 to 100 or 1 to 10 on the *strength* of the relationship. Figure 5-11 provides a list of possible metrics or factors to consider in establishing a metric on the relationship health.

The scorecard of Momentum Textiles in Irvine, California, provides a good example of how these questions and the information they generate can be used. The company has a partner relationship analytic on

1. How much money do you spend with this firm each year?

2. How long have your two firms been working together?

3. How critical is the firm's product or service to your own success?

4. How many other firms do you buy from that have the same products/services?

5. How unique are the qualities of this firm's products/services/people?

Figure 5-10. Questions to Consider When Rating Your Suppliers

1. Your report card or survey ratings of their performance.

2. Their report card or ratings of your performance.

3. How long your two firms have been working together.

4. Whether or not the firm works exclusively with your organization.

5. Personal contacts and friendships between individuals in your two firms.

6. Ties between the partner and other parts of your organization (i.e., corporate, other units, etc.).

7. The partner firm's knowledge of your organization and how it operates.

8. Political connections.

9. Difficulty in finding a replacement for this supplier/partner (from your perspective).

10. Difficulty in replacing you with another customer (from their perspective).

11. What percentage of revenue you provide for the partner firm.

Figure 5-11. Factors to Consider When Evaluating Your Relationships with Your Suppliers or Partners

its scorecard that measures its relationship with fabric mills that manufacture the products Momentum designs. By using this measure, Momentum was able to identify the vendors with whom there was a problem and the vendors that Momentum needed to work with to improve the relationship. The company has recently begun working with some new fabric mills in China and is beginning to establish trusting relationships with these firms. The Chinese mills are *high in importance* because they manufacture a large volume of Momentum's commodity fabrics, but the relationships are *not strong* yet because the firms have only been working together for a few years. Time zones and language/cultural barriers make improving the relationships somewhat challenging.

Regulatory Compliance: Measuring How You Meet Requirements

We are all expected to comply with various laws and regulations, and all organizations are overseen by various regulators. Nevertheless, problems with compliance can surface, sometimes unexpectedly. By the time a major problem is encountered, leaders do not need a scorecard to tell them something is wrong—it's already obvious. The purpose of the regulatory compliance metric is to prevent the unexpected by providing a future-focused measure of how your organization is doing at meeting or exceeding external requirements. Regulatory compliance has become an important concern for businesses over the last 10 years, a by-product of insider trading, falsified research results and audits, and assorted lies about corporate financial results. These unsavory and unpleasant aspects of the business world have increased the importance of regulatory compliance data on the executive scorecard.

Creating a Regulatory Compliance Analytic

The first step in constructing a regulatory compliance metric or analytic is to establish weights for each of the regulators that oversee your organization. Weights should be based on three factors:

- the amount of work required to meet the requirements,
- the severity of the consequences of violating the regulations (i.e., negative audit findings versus going to jail), and
- the importance of the factor being regulated to the overall business of the organization.

A chemical or water business would most probably give high weights to the EPA and other local environmental regulations. Similarly, a bank or investment firm would assign high weights to government mandated financial regulations.

The next step is to identify the measures that will go into the regulatory compliance analytic. This is a process, and any process analytic usually comprises a combination of input, process, output, and outcome measures. Each of these four factors needs to be weighted as well. Typically, there is a heavier weight put on the inputs and processes. Outcome measures are given a lower weight because they rarely occur in most organizations. Suggested weights and examples are shown in Figure 5-12.

Type of Metric	Weight	Examples
Inputs	25%	Completeness of data on regulations
		Extent to which regulations are up-to-date
		Knowledge of regulatory requirements
		Process for ensuring compliance has been documented
Process	35%	Objectivity of internal audits
		Thoroughness of internal audits
		Compliance with procedures linked to regulations
		Effectiveness of training on regulations/compliance
		Completion of milestones on regulatory compliance projects
		Consistency of audits, training, and other preventive approaches
		Process improvements
Outputs	30%	Repeat audit findings
		Accuracy and completeness of audit reports
		Quality and thoroughness of plans to remediate audit findings
		$ spent to comply with regulations
Outcomes	15%	Awards/recognition received related to regulations
		Citations, fines, violations
		Severity of fines and violations
		Gains or losses of certifications
		Decreased audit frequency
		Requests for benchmarking by other companies
		Audit scores by external regulators

Figure 5-12. Suggested Regulatory Compliance Factors and Their Weights

Chapter Summary

A management or executive scorecard would be incomplete without including a number of external measures of what is going on outside the organization that could have a major impact on its performance. Outside factors may be variables the organization has little or no control over but which could cause major shifts in other measures on the organization's scorecard. Most forward-looking organizations gather and review this type of external information, but they fail to quantify it on their scorecards. A scorecard becomes more comprehensive and useful if it includes the following types of external metrics:

- Brand image,
- Outside factors,
- Risks and threats,
- Relationships with suppliers and partners, and
- Regulatory compliance.

Organizations have traditionally gathered this type of data, but I have yet to see a scorecard in any major corporation that quantifies external metrics. Most of the time, this data is gathered periodically (usually annually) through some sort of audit or study. Typically, an organization hires a company to assess its emergency preparedness or to give its suppliers a report card. Instead of limiting this type of information to an occasional study, however, most organizations would benefit from including metrics addressing external factors on their scorecards. This is a sound recommendation because the external factors discussed in this chapter are just as critical to your organization's success as your own performance. Although many of these variables cannot be influenced by your organization, some of them can, and all of them are factors that need to be monitored on an ongoing basis. The scorecard becomes a much better analytical and decision-making tool if external measures are paired with your internal measures of company performance. Just as airplane pilots have a number of weather gauges on their dashboards, executives need external factors on their scorecards.

The next chapter focuses on developing meaningful people or human resource analytics. This is the section of the scorecard that is the least sophisticated and least refined in most organizations, even though it is probably the most important. Measuring and managing factors like employee satisfaction and intellectual capital is critical to success in today's business environment.

Key Points to Keep in Mind
About External Metrics and Analytics

☐ External factors can have a huge bearing on how an organization sets goals and develops strategies—and on its overall success.

☐ Most scorecards do not include measures of external factors such as image, politics, economic factors, competition, and other factors.

☐ A scorecard can become a much better management tool if external factors are tracked on a regular basis and reported as analytics along with other gauges.

☐ Some of the external factors that should be considered for scorecard metrics include image, risk/threats, supplier/partner performance, and meeting legal and regulatory requirements.

☐ Any one of these factors can bring an organization to its knees, so data on these factors should not be limited to an annual assessment. These variables need to be monitored and reported with the same frequency and precision as internal measures of company performance.

6

People Analytics: Measuring Your Most Important Asset

More and more European and North American countries are making a transition from manufacturing to service-based industries that require a different range of skills and knowledge. This evolution has spurred a change in how organizations rate the importance of their people as an integral part of organizational success. In manufacturing organizations, such as a steel mill or a paper mill, labor is not a major cost. In a software firm, government department, or airline, it is. In addition, the type of knowledge required of labor in manufacturing is quite different from that required in today's predominantly service-based industries. So is the importance of employee satisfaction. Several studies have shown strong links between employee satisfaction and outcomes like growth, profits, and loyal customers. In spite of these changes, people analytics remain the most unsophisticated set of metrics on most organization's scorecards.

If you compare what organizations are measuring today with what they measured 20 years ago, you will find that the metrics for measuring people have not changed much at all, and this makes them virtually useless. One notable exception to this can be found in the Gallup organization, which has used its research with hundreds of companies to determine the 12 most important factors to ask about on an employee satisfaction survey. The findings were published in an excellent book: *First Break All the Rules*. The downside to this breakthrough, however, is that the recommended survey is still a once-a-year survey, which does not take into account morale changes on a daily or even hourly basis. This chapter of *Beyond the Balanced Scorecard* shows an alternative methodology for measuring people.

Figure 6-1 lists the questions that should be answered by the human resource analytics you choose for your scorecard, and Figure 6-2 lists five basic people metrics that are discussed below: employee satisfaction, health and safety, ethics and diversity, human/intellectual capital (having people with the right mix of knowledge/skills), and communication effectiveness. Of course, not all organizations need all five of these metrics, but all are worth considering.

The questions that should be answered by the metrics in the human resources or people section of your scorecard are:

☐ How satisfied and engaged are our employees?

☐ How healthy and safe are our employees?

☐ How are we really doing on ethics and diversity?

☐ Do we have the right people with the right knowledge and skills?

☐ Are we effectively communicating with our people?

Figure 6-1. Questions Answered by Human Resource Analytics

Employee Satisfaction Analytic	Health & Safety Analytic	Ethics/Diversity Analytic	Human Capital Analytic	Communication Effectiveness Analytic

Figure 6-2. Basic Human Resources Analytics

Depending on the nature of the organization or the kind of business it is engaged in, the weight of each of these five individual analytics may vary quite a bit. For example, the Health & Safety metric should probably be given a high weight in a dangerous manufacturing company. The Ethics/Diversity Analytic should probably be heavily weighted in a company that has just lost several lawsuits related to diversity issues or in a company that has had to fire managers or supervisors for ethics violations. The three metrics that are always important in all types of organizations are Employee Satisfaction, Human Capital, and Communication. For illustrative purposes, some generic weights for the five sub-measures in the Human Resource Analytic are presented in Figure 6-3.

1. Employee Satisfaction	25%
2. Health & Safety	10%
3. Diversity and Ethics	15%
4. Human Capital	30%
5. Communication	20%

Figure 6-3. Suggested Weights for the 5 Sub-Metrics of the People Analytic

People Analytics is the section of the scorecard that can be applied to just about every organization. Regardless of whether you are designing a scorecard for a hospital, school, service company, government organization, military facility, or manufacturing company, people or HR metrics tend to be the same. Other sections of the scorecard vary greatly, but the five sub-metrics listed in Figure 6-3 should be of concern to any organization that employs a great number of people and should be systematically used to gauge how those people are doing. Smaller organizations, for example, those with 12 or fewer people, do not necessarily need people metrics on their scorecards. This does not mean that people metrics should be dismissed or ignored; it simply means that data can be gathered a different way—perhaps by talking with your people on a regular basis. Let's take a look at each of these sub-metrics in more detail.

People Metric #1: Employee Satisfaction

Gallup calls a happy or satisfied employee an "engaged employee." Regardless of what you want to call it, it is important for organizations to know how many of their employees get up each morning and dread coming to work and how many get up each morning looking forward to a new workday. Most organizations don't have a clue about this. When someone "goes postal" or quits after making a big scene, coworkers usually know why, but most managers are shocked. There is just as much mystery with respect to the millionaires who do not have to work at all but come to work and stay, not because of a paycheck but because they like the work.

The examples above are somewhat extreme, because most people do not fit either profile. Most people, however, are either satisfied or dissatisfied with their jobs and are either engaged or not engaged to them. Figure 6-4 lists some reasons organizations should care about this.

---

1. Satisfied employees are much more productive, giving 110 percent versus just enough to avoid being fired.

2. Satisfied employees tend not to steal and cheat the company.

3. Satisfied employees feel more free to take risks and be innovative.

4. Satisfied employees refer their friends when a job opens up, a good way to save time and money on recruiting prescreening.

5. Satisfied employees tend to treat customers and suppliers better, leading to greater loyalty and profits.

Figure 6-4. Five Good Reasons to Keep Your Employees Happy

Becoming an Employer of Choice

A common theme in organizational vision statements is the desire to be the "first choice for customers, shareholders, and employees." In fact, if I had a dollar for every organization that mentions in its strategic plan or vision statement that it wants to be an "employer of choice," I could retire a lot sooner. But "employer of choice" has become one of those nice vanilla catch phrases used by companies that have not put much thought into their strategic plans. Having a good strategic plan requires much more than buzzwords. It means following the lead of companies like Starbucks, Southwest Airlines, Ritz-Carlton, and the Container Store, which have made being a great place to work a major part of their success strategy. These companies put a lot of effort into finding and keeping the best employees, and they credit much of their success to this strategy.

Most big companies and government organizations have a long way to go toward becoming great places to work. The healthcare industry is probably the worst. In a recent survey by the American Medical Association, 75 percent of doctors reported that practicing medicine is less satisfying than in the past, and two-thirds of these doctors claimed they would advise their children not to work in the medical field. That is a pretty sad statement about what used to be considered an honorable and desirable profession. Some hospitals and clinics are bucking the trend, however, and do seem to care about the morale of their staffs. They are finding that high morale pays off in many ways. In fact, employee satisfaction was the foundation of the turnaround strategy of CEO Al Stubblefield, who led his Baptist Hospital in Pensacola, Florida, to win a Baldrige Award a few years ago.

If you, as an employer, believe in the value of creating an environment that is a great place to work, your greatest challenge is to figure out how to know when you've arrived and how to measure your progress along the way. Consider the following approaches.

How *Fortune* Magazine Picks the 100 Best Employers

Each year, *Fortune* Magazine runs an issue that lists and ranks the 100 best companies to work for. Many of these companies are household names that you would expect to see on the list, like Starbucks, Cisco, and Microsoft, but among the top 25 listed, there are probably more companies that most people have never heard of. In fact, only one of the top 5 companies for 2006 (Wegman's Food Markets) would be classified as a large business.

The rankings are far from a popularity contest: *Fortune* uses very specific metrics to establish the scores of best employers. Two-thirds of the selection criteria are based on levels of employee satisfaction measured via survey. The remaining one-third of the score is determined by special services and programs offered to employees, unique benefits, and hard statistics such as turnover, job growth, the number of job applicants per year, training hours, and average pay for professionals and hourly employees.

Each of the companies profiled in the magazine does something unusual that makes it stand out. For example, the company that ranked #1 in 2006 is a medical research firm called Genentech. Along with working for a company that has a noble cause (fighting cancer), 95 percent of the 8,000 employees are shareholders, and the value of the stock has soared in recent years. For W. L. Gore & Associates, the company ranked #5 on the magazine's list, the path to "best" was radically different. The company has no bosses, job titles, or organization charts. Now that sounds like a real innovation!

Creating an Employee Satisfaction Analytic

A lot of smart people have been involved in determining the criteria *Fortune* uses to identify the best employers in the United States, so it is logical to use their knowledge and findings to help construct a good employee satisfaction metric. One company I worked with wanted its metric to mirror the factors *Fortune* looks at, including how it weighs each of the sub-measures in its employee satisfaction analytic. The "employer of choice" metric this company constructed was made up of the sub-metrics shown in Figure 6-5.

☐ Employee satisfaction survey	65%
☐ Turnover	7%
☐ Job growth	7%
☐ Training hours	7%
☐ Applicants	7%
☐ Average salary/pay	7%

Figure 6-5. Employee Satisfaction Sub-Metrics Used by *Fortune* Magazine to Determine the Best Employers in America

There are several problems, however, with the example shown in Figure 6-5 as an employee satisfaction analytic. First of all, a number of the sub-metrics are probably going to be annual measures—e.g., the satisfaction survey, job growth, and average salary. A further problem is that too much weight is put on the employee survey, and surveys are not known to be the most reliable measure of employee morale. While it is a great idea to build on the research done by *Fortune* to create an employee satisfaction analytic, *Fortune's* approach is more suitable to an annual audit. The magazine evaluates whether or not a company is a great place to work once a year; what we are looking for is an *ongoing* metric that can be tracked on at least a monthly basis. Note, however, that many of the factors examined by *Fortune*, such as whether or not you offer flexible scheduling, daycare, a fitness center, sabbaticals, and stock options, will not change within a given year.

Some Metrics to Consider for an Employee Satisfaction Analytic

In the last 10 years or so, some organizations have come up with some interesting and innovative sub-metrics for their employee satisfaction analytic. Consider the list in Figure 6-6 as possibilities and idea-starters, but be careful not to go overboard by trying to use all of them at once. Choose no more than 4 to 6 of these to put together your analytic.

As with constructing any analytic, it is important to try and select a variety of sub-metrics that represent past, present, and future perspectives. For example:

- turnover is a *past* metric;
- surveys and complaints are a *present*-focused metric; and
- new services introduced or new employees that are referred by your existing employees are leading indicators or *future*-focused metrics.

One measure in the Employee Satisfaction Analytic of two recent clients is a measure of daily or weekly stress. The first organization that came up with this idea was the Army's Strategic Missile Defense Command in Huntsville, Alabama, whose people filled in their time sheets electronically once a week. The organization decided to add a question at the end of the time sheet that asked people to describe what kind of a week they had on a scale of 1 to 10. A rating of 1 indicated a week so bad that the person was probably close to going postal. A 10 rating indicated a week so good that the person would continue working there even after winning $10 million in the lottery.

The other client, the Los Angeles Bureau of Sanitation, came up with a daily low-tech version of the stress metric. Staff members in the Information Technology area dropped a red, yellow, or green marble in a vase at the end of each day, depending on what kind of day they had. (At first, glass jars were used, but the company found that seeing how other people had rated their day influenced which color of marble

☐ Hours worked per week

☐ Average # of e-mails received per employee

☐ % of time spent in meetings

☐ Employee aggravation index
- Changes in reporting relationships/bosses/org. chart
- Office/work location moves
- Changes in benefits
- New software
- New procedures
- Commuting/parking difficulties
- Amount of travel
- Meetings
- New coworkers

☐ Monthly pop-up surveys to a sample of employees

☐ Monthly focus groups with a sample of employees

☐ Employee complaints and severity

☐ Turnover index (turnover $\times$ seniority $\times$ job level)

☐ Job opening filled with external candidates vs. internal candidates

☐ Weekly or daily stress measure

☐ Casual absenteeism

☐ % of employees on stress-related medication or on leave

☐ New employees referred by existing employees

☐ New services or benefits for employees

☐ Employee use of new benefits and services

☐ Increased or decreased supervision/oversight

Figure 6-6. Metrics to Consider When Evaluating Employee Satisfaction

someone dropped in the jar.) The marbles were sorted and counted and graphed daily, providing a daily statistic on morale and stress for very little cost. The system even made it easy to see what was going on in different areas, because there were different vases for each group or department. When a department noticed a lot of red marbles, the supervisor went around and talked to people about what had happened the day before. So the marbles, which were initially used only to gauge stress and morale, also had a side benefit—managers and supervisors began talking to their people more often.

People Metric #2: Employee Health and Safety

Manufacturing organizations have been focused on the safety of their employees for quite some time. However, the metrics commonly tracked are simply numbers of lost-time accidents. In other words, someone has to get hurt for the metric to move. Although this lagging indicator is certainly important, a measure of an organization's health and safety should encompass much more, and even service companies and government organizations need to be concerned about employee safety. Injuries like carpal tunnel and back problems, neither of which can be classified as accidents, cost such organizations millions of dollars each year.

Employers have also become increasingly concerned about the health of their employees. Health insurance costs continue to escalate, and a number of health-related concerns have prompted some employers to set policies regarding unhealthy behaviors. Obesity is one of the major concerns that have influenced employers to take action. Although it is probably illegal to not hire people because they are grossly overweight, employers do it all the time. One of the largest and oldest temporary labor firms in the country, for example, had a secret code on interview forms to signify that someone was fat.

Smoking is another concern for employers. Nationwide Insurance recently made an announcement that all employees who smoke had 30 days to quit smoking or lose their jobs. The company offered free programs to help smokers quit, but it refused to back down on the threat to fire smokers if they continued to smoke. The policy included blood tests, which would detect noncompliance.

The subject was raised at a workshop I recently conducted, which was attended by a group of Nationwide employees as well as employees of other companies. During lunch, one Nationwide employee, a smoker, explained the new policy to the rest of us and asked what we thought of it. He commented that he had been with the company for more than 10 years, that he smoked only at home or away from work, and that he thought it was grossly unfair for the company to issue an edict that controlled his behavior outside of work. "What's next?" he asked. "Will companies fire people if they eat red meat, drink alcohol, or don't exercise on a regular basis?" He did bring up some good points about how far a company can go in controlling the behavior of its employees.

The general feeling of the people at the same lunch table, which included a couple of other Nationwide employees, was that the policy was legal, ethical, and a smart business decision for Nationwide. There is very convincing data that smokers are more prone to all sorts of health problems, so a company should be able to choose not to employ (or even to dismiss) smokers.

Regardless of your stance on this issue, Nationwide is certainly not unique in this quest to make employees healthier. We have a long way to go in this arena, however. Even hospitals, which should lead the pack in encouraging the health of their employees, serve horribly unhealthy food in their cafeterias: hamburgers, fries, macaroni and cheese, pizza dripping with grease, and deep-fried fish smothered in tartar sauce. You can always opt for a salad, but it is usually iceberg lettuce, which has no nutritional value, and the dressings are so loaded with fat that you are better off with the pizza.

Creating a Health and Safety Analytic

Your first step in creating a Health and Safety Analytic should be to decide how important health and safety are. Many organizations put equal weight on each factor. If your organization has a lot of safety hazards, you might want to make the weights 70 percent safety and 30 percent health, or 60/40. After deciding on the relative weight of these two factors, you need to identify the individual measures that should go into each metric. Keep in mind that both the safety and health metrics should be properly balanced and include *leading* and *lagging* indicators.

Safety Metrics. Most good safety metrics I have seen look like the example shown in Figure 6-7. This example puts half of the weight on the leading indicators, which should be of more concern to managers than the lagging indicators, which measure the past.

# of accidents × severity (1–10)	50%
Safety training test scores	10%
Near misses	10%
Safety audit scores	20%
Behavior/protective equipment use	10%

Figure 6-7. Example Safety Metric

Health Metrics. A measure that tells you about the health of your workforce is more of a challenge, and I have worked with only a handful of organizations that have developed such metrics. A couple of examples that will give you some idea of variables that can be included in a health metric are shown in Figures 6-8 and 6-9.

Health incidents × severity (1–10)	20%
Data from employee physicals	40%
Absenteeism	10%
Participation in health fairs	10%
Healthy lifestyle training	10%

Figure 6-8. Employee Health Metric—Example #1

The metrics with the most integrity in the example shown in Figure 6-8 is data on health incidents (i.e., surgeries, hospitalizations, etc.) and from annual physicals. Statistics on resting heart rate, blood pressure, weight, cholesterol, and other factors provide excellent and reliable data on the overall health of people. Averages would be compared to health standards to determine if results are red, yellow, or green. The other three factors in the health analytic are given a minor weight because they are not the best indicators of employee health. People are sometimes absent just because they need a mental health day. Many healthy employees may simply not be interested in participating in company-sponsored health fairs or training.

A hospital I worked with created an employee health metric that was even simpler than the one illustrated in Figure 6-8. The hospital administrators did not want to include data from employee physicals and health incidents because they felt it would be too intrusive to collect such data. The design of the hospital's health metric is shown in Figure 6-9.

Lifestyle/diet questionnaire	35%
Cafeteria food sales	10%
Health training test scores	15%
Participation in exercise/sports	10%
Employees who get annual physical	30%

Figure 6-9. Employee Health Metric—Example #2

People Metric #3: Ethics and Diversity

Ethics and diversity are two topics that everyone talks about these days, but most HR departments, which should be addressing these concerns, do not have good diversity or ethics measures on their scorecards. To make matters worse, I know of only one big corporation with a diversity metric on its CEO's scorecard. Moreover, the organization has lost several lawsuits because of diversity problems, and the inclusion of diversity metrics on its executive-level scorecard can probably be attributed to this history, at least in part. A few forward-thinking organizations have vice presidents in charge of ethics, but none of them seem to have any good metrics to tell them how the organization is performing in this area.

Attention to ethics and diversity issues can be very important from a business standpoint. If your company has a reputation as a great place to work for women or minorities, you have a real advantage. Mary Kay Cosmetics recognized this some time ago and even has a mission statement that includes the following phrase: *To give unlimited opportunity to women.* Union Bank of California has also recognized this and is consistently rated as one of the best companies for minorities and women. At the Santa Clara Valley Water District in San

Jose, diversity is second nature: The workforce is about as varied as the United Nations, from executive row right on down to the worker level. Those rare organizations that really do an excellent job on diversity may not even need diversity metrics on their scorecards—the gauge would always be green. But for the rest of you, it is likely that there is room for improvement, and you should have a measure to track that improvement.

Many people in a position of power are tempted to abuse that power, but this aspect of human nature seems to have become worse over the last decade or two. In the last 10 years, we have seen some major corporations disappear, or at least have their executives carted off to jail, because of ethics problems. Every one of these companies had policies, audits, a code of ethics, and ethics training. Executives monitored the doctored financial results on their corporate dashboards and felt good because the gauges were all green ... until the FBI showed up. Today, many companies are busy working to ensure compliance with the new Sarbanes-Oxley regulations that are supposed to make companies more ethical. Yet, this is unlikely to do much to control unethical behavior among some organizational leaders. What it will do is make it easier to convict them when they get caught.

None of the companies (including Enron, HealthSouth, and WorldCom) that made the headlines for their unethical practices had an ethics metric that they monitored on a regular basis. They all did things to try to ensure ethical behavior, but had no data on how well those strategies were working. That is like waiting to see if you have a heart attack to see how well your new exercise and drug therapy program is working. By the time you get some data, it's too late.

Were there signs of trouble in these companies before they got into big trouble? You bet! They just chose not to measure the signs, or to ignore them. No company goes bad overnight. Going bad is a process that starts with small infractions that escalate as people learn they can get away with more and more.

Developing an Ethics Analytic

The key to any useful performance metric is that it alerts you to problems when there is still time to correct them. Ethics is a fairly complex aspect of an organization's performance that cannot be measured by counting a single statistic. A company that counts the percentage of employees who attended ethics training when they first joined the company and does nothing else has clearly missed the point. (The guys from Enron probably all attended ethics training classes at some stage in their careers, but something obviously went awry somewhere, no?)

So if a single measure does not really tell an organization how it is doing on ethics, how does one construct a good ethics analytic that detects minor problems so that they can be easily corrected before someone goes to jail, gets fired, or ends up on the front page of a newspaper? Ethics Analytics that I have helped some organizations develop in the last few years usually consist of five types of sub-measures, shown in Figure 6-10.

1. Employee knowledge of right and wrong

2. Perceptions about what really goes on (the real values)

3. Deployment of programs designed to ensure ethical behavior

4. Employee behavior

5. Outcomes (could be positive or negative)

Figure 6-10. Five Sub-Measures for Ethics Analytics

Most organizations put a lot of weight on the measures of behavior and outcomes even though these are lagging metrics. By the time you have behavior problems or outcomes—such as someone being charged with a crime—you are already in trouble. Employee perceptions about ethical behavior and values in the organization are also a strong indicator, assuming the survey data has integrity. One client actually surveys customers, employees, and suppliers to ask them how they perceive the ethics of the organization. This gives the data a more complete picture of how people outside and inside view its ethics. In a typical Ethics Analytic, the 5 sub-metrics are weighted as shown in Figure 6-11.

Figure 6-11 shows a well-balanced analytic because 45 percent of its sub-metrics are leading and 55 percent are lagging. An ethics mea-

Employee Knowledge	10%
Perceptions	25%
Processes/Programs	15%
Behavior	20%
Outcomes	30%

Figure 6-11. Suggested Weightings of Sub-Metrics for Ethics Analytic

sure like this one would probably have done a good job of predicting problems at Arthur Andersen before things got out of hand. There would have been changes in perceptions, confusion about what is really right and wrong, and subtle changes in behavior that occurred before people started doing things that were really illegal. Now the hard question is how you actually measure the five variables listed in Figure 6-10. The following section describes each one in more detail.

Measuring Knowledge of Right and Wrong. The first sub-metric should tell leaders whether people *really* know right from wrong. Counting how many people attend ethics training might be part of this index, but I would not put much weight on that. Ethics training is usually mandatory, and many employees report forgetting the content within an hour of completing the training.

Making ethics training interesting is quite a challenge. One successful method comes from Sandia Labs, which hired Dilbert creator Scott Adams to develop its ethics training. There is always a waiting list to get into the courses, and this alone attests to their impact. My colleague Denise Shields and I developed an ethics workshop that includes a series of video vignette situations that are commonly encountered at work. Teams must decide on the right course of action, and the answer is never black and white—the title of the program is *Shades of Gray*.

Making sure that employees know right from wrong is the first step in creating an ethical organization, and a good measure for ethics training is what percentage of attendees can pass a test at the end. One client actually administers such a test at the end of the training and three months later.

Measuring Perceptions Regarding Ethics. The second type of measure that goes into the Ethics Analytic is a measure of people's perceptions. Employees might clearly know right from wrong, but standard practice in an organization may be to look the other way when behavior is in violation of the rules. In some companies, for example, many employees use the copy machine for personal stuff, surf the web, take home office supplies from time to time, and take a day off when not really sick. These may be small violations, but they set a bad precedent that can easily lead to worse things.

A good way of measuring perceptions about what really goes on is to anonymously survey a sample of employees periodically, or to hold a focus group off site. One client picks about 50 people a month to survey and asks questions about the extent to which they trust senior management and whether or not behavior in the company is consistent with company rules and values. Another client does a survey once a quarter but surveys customers and suppliers as well as employees. The company uses an outside firm to conduct the survey to ensure anonymity. The issue of anonymity is important: Without anonymity, it is unlikely that suppliers will say anything bad about your firm if they want to continue to get your business. And customers may also be reluctant to be honest if they want to continue to get those Super Bowl tickets slipped to them each year.

Ethics Process Metrics. The third sub-metric in an Ethics Analytic should be a measure of the processes you have in place to ensure ethical behavior from your people. Compliance with Sarbanes-Oxley would certainly be something to consider measuring in this index. The Council for Ethical Organizations has developed a series of criteria and standards for evaluating the ethics programs in organizations. The model is similar to the Baldrige Award model or the Capability Maturity Model developed by the Software Engineering Institute. Seven aspects of your approach to ethics and compliance are evaluated and scored, as shown in Figure 6-12.[1]

One way of constructing a process metric is to have an annual assessment performed by a group like the Council for Ethical Organi-

---

1. Developed by the Council for Ethical Organizations

1. Oversight and support. How much autonomy does this function have, and do people receive adequate resources to do their job?

2. Compliance Officer and office. Do you have an Ethics VP or equivalent and a staff to support him or her?

3. Code and supporting policies. Do you have a written code of ethics and related policies, and how comprehensive and current are they?

4. Internal reporting. What sort of metrics do you track to evaluate your performance in the area of ethics and compliance?

5. Education and training. How thorough, effective, and frequent is the training you do on ethics and compliance?

6. Internal controls and corrective actions. What systems and processes do you have in place to prevent problems and correct them when they occur?

7. Periodic program assessment. How frequently and thoroughly do you evaluate the effectiveness of your ethics and compliance program/effort?

Figure 6-12. Criteria and Standards for Evaluating Ethics Programs

zations. This is exactly what Palomar Pomerado Hospitals does as part of its ethics metric. The score received from this assessment gives hospital administrators a way to track progress in developing and deploying a comprehensive ethics and compliance program. The downside to this as a metric is that it is annual. Therefore, other more frequent metrics need to be tracked. One company I work with has an ethics process analytic that looks like the one shown in Figure 6-13. Three of the four sub-measures in the analytic shown here move every month, and 30 percent of the analytic moves only once a year, when a new audit score is entered in the equation.

Training attendance	25%
Communication	35%
Cycle time for investigations	10%
Annual ethics audit score	30%

Figure 6-13. Ethics Process Analytic—Example #1

Another client has developed an ethics process metric that is a measure of the ethics projects/programs that are being developed and implemented. At the time I worked with this client, the company was in the process of working on four programs/projects. Within each of these projects was a measure of budget, schedule/milestones, and quality of deliverables. Figure 6-14 shows how this client weighted its ethics projects.

Project 1: Ethics policy/code	25%
Project 2: Whistle-blower program	30%
Project 3: Update ethics training	15%
Project 4: Communication strategy	30%

Figure 6-14. Ethics Process Analytic—Example #2

Each of the four project metrics shown in Figure 6-14 indicated performance as red, yellow, or green, and if a project was not showing green, management could drill down into the details to determine if this signaled a problem related to quality, schedule, or budget. A process metric like this one works well in a company that does not yet have (but really needs) an ethics/compliance program. In an organization that already has a complete and mature process, the example shown in Figure 6-13 is probably a better metric.

Another possibility for an ethics process measure is a metric called the "Corporate Governance Quotient." This metric was created by a consulting/information company called Intuitional Shareholder Services. The CGQ is an analytic itself, made up of an evaluation of 63 factors categorized into four focus areas:

1. Board of Directors
2. Audit
3. Anti-takeover Provisions
4. Executive and Director Compensation.

Each company in the 8,000 companies that ISS has in its database is given a score on the CGQ, based mostly on publicly disclosed information, press releases, and corporate websites. This data is then verified by ISS analysts. The results show how a company scores overall, as well as how it ranks within a given industry. The great thing about the CGQ is that it allows you to set targets based on how you rank against other companies and specifically against industry peers. The bad thing about this metric is that it is nowhere near as thorough as the score provided by the Council for Ethical Organizations. On the other hand, an ethics index that includes external statistics like the CGQ is likely to have a lot more credibility than one that is based solely on self-reported data.

Measuring Ethical Behavior. The fourth sub-metric in a good Ethics Analytic is a measure of employee behavior. This is different from a measure of opinions or perceptions; this gauge tracks behaviors that are consistent or inconsistent with your stated values and code of ethics.

Most people police their own behavior, but if you fail to notice your own inappropriate behavior, your peers are more than happy to point it out and make you cough up a dollar. The company takes a daily count of how many dollars were collected in the meeting rooms and enters that into their scorecard database. Another measure of unethical behavior is how many people are "written up" for breaking the rules, particularly serious infractions such as lying to a customer, leaving work early on a regular basis, or falsifying an expense report. Each incident is coded, based on the degree of severity and the number of write-ups for the same behavior.

Measure of Outcomes. The fifth and final sub-measure in an Ethics Analytic should be a measure of outcomes. Outcomes are different from behaviors. Behaviors lead to outcomes, but behavior is what people do, whereas an outcome is the result of the behavior. For example, driving 80 miles an hour is a behavior; getting a $250 speeding ticket may be an outcome. One client measures the outcomes shown in Figure 6-15.

In the example shown in Figure 6-11, there is a heavy weight on the outcomes because it would be hard to say you are doing a good job on ethics if you are on the front page of the newspaper because your executives are doing something illegal. Outcomes for ethics are

---

Negative Outcomes:
- ☐ Violations of regulations relating to ethics (# and severity)
- ☐ Whistle-blower reports (# and severity)
- ☐ Negative press coverage concerning ethics issues
- ☐ Internet chat room/blogs concerning ethics
- ☐ Lawsuits
- ☐ Employee complaints
- ☐ Dismissals for ethics problems (and dismissing higher-level employees counts much more).

Positive outcomes that move the gauge the other way might include:
- ☐ Commendations
- ☐ Awards
- ☐ Positive press coverage
- ☐ Support of charity and community groups
- ☐ Benchmarking of your ethics program by other companies

Figure 6-15. Example of Ethics Outcomes Measured by One Company

kind of like outcomes in a safety analytic: Most are negative. A number of my clients have designed the safety metric so that if there is ever a fatality or serious injury, the whole metric turns red. This same approach makes sense for an Ethics Analytic.

Developing a Diversity Analytic

Unlike ethics, most organizations have some kind of measure of diversity. It is usually somewhere in HR, but at least there is a metric. The problem is that most diversity metrics are limited to a statistic on the percentage of nonwhite males in the total population of employees. This may be one of the things that gets measured, but by itself, it really does not tell an organization how it is doing on diversity.

I recently worked with Lawrence Berkley National Laboratory to help the lab develop a better measure of diversity for the Lab Director's scorecard. Looking around the lab did not reveal much of a problem with diversity. In fact, if you had less than 2 tattoos, only 4 piercings, and a normal haircut, you wouldn't blend in. However, there did seem to be an abnormal number of older white males with gray hair and beards, so there was clearly some room for improvement. Because we were developing an Ethics Analytic at the same time, we decided to design parallel metrics. We came up with the four types of sub-metrics in the Diversity Analytic shown in Figure 6-16 and described in detail in the following paragraphs.

Inputs	15%
Perceptions	25%
Process	20%
Outputs/Outcomes	40%

Figure 6-16. Example of a Diversity Analytic, with Weights

Diversity Input Metrics. Harry, the Diversity Manager at the lab, explained to me that part of the reason organizations like Berkley Labs don't have good diversity is that most scientists and engineers are white males. He further explained that part of the problem is that managers like to hire people who went to the same schools they went to.

One of Harry's strategies to improve the number of nonwhite male applicants was to look in nontraditional countries and schools for candidates. So one of the input measures we came up with was the diversity of people applying for jobs at the laboratory. Another input metric was the number of new places that jobs were advertised. Another strategy that the lab was employing to increase the number of women and minority applicants was to offer more internships to a more diverse assortment of people and to work with colleges and universities and even high schools to encourage kids to major in science and/or engineering.

Perceptions Regarding Diversity. The second dimension of the Diversity Analytic was a measure of perceptions or opinions. The culture of the laboratory was very strong, and it had long been dominated by what Harry called "the graybeard scientists." Perceptions of some employees were that if you were not one of the graybeards, or not a scientist, you were a second-class citizen at the lab. Perceptions of employees as well as contractors and job candidates were measured by anonymous survey. The survey included questions about the culture of the laboratory, with a number of the questions specifically focused on diversity.

Measuring Diversity Programs. It was also important to come up with process metrics as part of the Diversity Analytic. The purpose of this measure was to tell management if the organization was doing all the things it was supposed to do to have a good diversity program. For example, the diversity process metric for one government client included a type of audit score like the one mentioned above for the ethics process metric developed by the Council for Ethical Organizations (refer back to Figure 6-11). There are similar standards for what a good affirmative action or diversity program ought to look like. Even though this was an annual assessment, it was a good evaluation of the progress the lab was making in having a more comprehensive diversity program. The lab got points for communication, plans, training, and other things.

Another part of the process metric was progress being made on projects designed to improve diversity. Each project was weighted and measured based on schedule, budget, and the quality of deliverables. Projects or activities included job fairs, succession planning, diversity celebrations, profiles in the newsletter, and other things. Process measures may also include measures of behavior. For example, one of my clients has a big Cinco de Mayo party each year. The number and diversity of people that attend such events might be a good behavior measure. If only Mexicans attend, it may signal a diversity problem.

Diversity Outputs and Outcomes. Outputs and outcomes are measures of statistics such as those listed in Figure 6-17.

According to Harry from Berkley Labs, what often happens in organizations is that they can recruit women and minorities to fill jobs, but keeping them is another matter altogether. They don't stay long because they perceive that the culture really does not embrace diversity and that opportunities are limited. Hence, turnover and how long people stay is a good outcome metric. People are unlikely to reveal the real reason they are leaving, but if you see that women or

□ Diversity of new hires

□ Diversity of the senior leadership team

□ Diversity by job level and department/function

□ Promotion rates of nonwhite males

□ Diversity of committees and project teams

□ Awards received relating to diversity

□ Benchmarking of your diversity program

□ Positive or negative press coverage relating to diversity

□ Turnover and reasons for leaving

□ Average employment length of nonwhite male employees

□ New employees coming from referrals from existing employees

□ $ in scholarships or internships to specific schools

Figure 6-17. Examples of Statistics to Measure Diversity
Output and Outcomes

Hispanic employees in technical jobs are leaving at a rate double that for white males, this probably indicates a diversity problem.

A common output diversity metric is to compare the diversity of your employee base to the diversity of the local community. For example, one school district I worked with is located in a community that is about 60 percent Hispanic, but about 80 percent of the school district's employees are white. The solution is not as simple as having 60 percent Hispanic employees if most of them are hired as janitors and groundskeepers. Instead, a measure that should be given higher weight is the diversity of the board and senior management. Most school boards are still almost all old white guys with perhaps one token woman or minority. The same is true of executive row in many corporations and government/military organizations. An example of a Diversity output/outcome metric is shown in Figure 6-18.

The bottom line on diversity is that it is a complex dimension of organizational performance. Some organizations have never had a problem with it and don't need to measure it. However, for many big

Workforce Diversity	50%
Overall	*40%*
Senior Management	*60%*
New Hires Diversity	15%
Awards/Recognition	10%
Turnover Index*	25%

*The turnover index or metric would be a figure that included the rank or level of the person leaving, the length of his or her employment, and demographics.

Figure 6-18. Example Diversity Output/Outcome Analytic

corporations, there is still much progress to be made, and a good Diversity Analytic will help tell senior management if any progress is really being made.

People Metric #4: Human Capital

An article recently in a popular business magazine suggested that 80 percent of corporate value is determined by nonfinancial assets such as intellectual capital. Ideas, knowledge, and competencies are the principal assets in a company that separate it from its competitors. Some aspects of intellectual capital—such as patents, product designs, and other tangible assets—are easily measurable, but the value of an experienced account executive who has built trusting relationships with many big customers is hard to quantify. Losing a person like this can be devastating. Hiring someone with the potential to develop similar skills can be invaluable. For these reason and many others, it makes sense to try to measure the strength of the human assets in your organization. A measure of human capital should move to the right every time you bring in a new employee, and move to the left every time someone leaves. But what does this really mean?

One of Microsoft's major business strategies is to hire the smartest people in the world. That sounds like a winning strategy, but how does the company know if it has accomplished that goal? Measuring human assets, after all, is a complicated process. What makes this even more difficult is that some people don't blossom right away. Suppose you hire Randy to work as an assistant in marketing, and he turns into one of your most innovative marketing people. Hopefully, Randy will get promoted, but sometimes promotion opportunities are limited, and unless you take the time and effort to quantify the value that Randy brings to the company, you might miss out on a golden opportunity. If Randy is not promoted, there is a chance he might feel underappreciated. He may leave or may lose interest in performing well.

It is equally important to quantify the absence of value. Sometimes, this can be a tricky proposition. Every organization has some percentage of deadwood, including in senior management, but trying to put data about this on the scorecard could become a legal and political nightmare. The next sections of this chapter present some ideas on what can go into a measure of your human assets or capital, along with some advice on metrics to avoid.

What Makes an Employee Valuable?

There are many qualities that make an employee valuable to an employer:

- *Specific knowledge and skill.* These are the obvious qualities, which are required to perform important tasks, for example, the skill to repair an expensive piece of equipment or detailed knowledge about how the military funding process works.
- *Interpersonal knowledge and skills, or nontechnical abilities*—for example, the ability to make a convincing presentation, or mediate a conflict, or motivate a team, all of which are valuable skills for managers or supervisors.
- *Intelligence or abilities.* These are characteristics employees have when they first come through the door. They are not a measure of specific knowledge and skills.
- *Relationships.* Some of your seasoned employees have probably developed trusting relationships with other employees and managers, customers, and vendors or partners. Relationships take years to develop and are the key to getting many things done at work.

The big challenge with all four of these dimensions is to quantify the value of each individual employee in a way that is accurate and meaningful.

Mostly Worthless Human Capital Metrics

Although most organizations are concerned about the intellectual assets of their people, most attempts to develop a human capital metric are a miserable failure. The typical measures that go into such an index are discussed in the following sections.

Training Hours. The logic chain here is that if we continue to invest in training and developing our employees, they will maintain their knowledge and skills at the highest level. But there are some big leaps in logic here. First of all, measuring the number of butts sitting in chairs at a training session is not a measure of knowledge and skill acquisition. Rather, it is a measure of how many people sat in how many classrooms for how many hours. In the real world, even that metric is often inaccurate. The training sign-in sheet is usually passed around in the morning. Some people don't come back after lunch because they have already signed in.

A second problem is that much of what gets called "training" is not training but talking. *Listening to someone talk while they show Power-Point slides is not training.* The third problem with this measure is that it does not include an assessment of whether or not the content covered in the training is even relevant to the job a person is doing.

It is tempting to measure training hours because the data is so easy to track, however, the type of data being tracked does not really measure the knowledge and skills of employees. In fact, some of the most competent people in organizations don't go to training—they are too busy doing meaningful, productive work.

Completion of "Individual Development Plans." Most large companies and nonprofit organizations have an annual process called Individual Development Planning (IDP) during which an employee sits down with his or her boss and decides what knowledge and skills should be worked on for the following year. This is actually a good idea, but the execution is usually flawed. The product of most IDPs is a list of conferences or workshops the employee wants to attend. If the employee lists four courses and attends all four, the score on the IDP is 100 percent. What this number does not measure is whether the employee really learned a new skill or mastered a new subject or content.

Certifications. Many fields require some form of certification—a piece of paper stating that the person holding it has attained competence in a particular field. For example, you can become a Certified Public Accountant, Registered Nurse, Certified Financial Planner, or certified welder.

The problem with counting these certifications as a measure of competence is that they are not. There are countless incompetent people out there with pieces of paper saying they are certified, but most of these people passed certification tests that measured their ability to memorize rather than their ability to perform. If the certification test actually requires the person to perform job tasks (i.e., fly a plane), it is a good measure of competence, but passing most certification tests requires nothing more than memorizing a bunch of rules, facts, and principles. In other words, the tests assess specific knowledge but not skills. People study for the exams, pass them, and then mostly forget what they learned. Whether or not they become competent in their field depends a lot on experience, intelligence, and further training and mentoring. Certifications are like training hours—they're easy to count, but they are not very revealing as a metric.

Developing a Human Capital Analytic

Quite a few organizations put some sort of human capital metric on their scorecards, but most are pretty rudimentary and do not capture the real value of their people. Salespeople or engineers that are superstars tend to get rated the same as people who are mediocre.

What this gauge or metric ought to tell you is whether or not you have the right number of people in the right jobs with the right knowledge and skills to do today's and tomorrow's work. A Human Capital Analytic should also tell you when people are likely to retire, so you can develop good recruiting and training plans for new staff. The most important metric that should be included in your Human

Capital Analytic is a measure of the skills and knowledge level of your employees. This is also the most difficult to measure objectively. The major sub-metrics that should be considered for a Human Capital Analytic are shown in Figure 6-19, and the following paragraphs describe each analytic in more detail.

Headcount vs. Need	15%
Average age of Employees	15%
Knowledge/Skill Index	70%
Experience	*40%*
Performance	*20%*
Knowledge/Skill	*40%*

Figure 6-19. Example of an Ideal Human Capital Analytic

Headcount. Headcount versus need and average age are both objective statistics that are easy to count. Having open positions that have not been filled causes a gap in the organization's human resources. You might want to consider putting a multiplier on the headcount factor, with higher-level positions counting much more. For example, a hospital I worked with did not have a Human Resources Director for more than a year. This caused a bigger gap than if the hospital had been missing a clerk in the billing department or a lower-level staff member.

Having too many employees can be just as much of a problem, and often makes this gauge red. General Motors, for example, currently has many more people than its workload demands, so it needs to trim its employee base to bring its human capital metric back into the green. As a result, GM is offering $140,000 severance packages to hourly workers to try to reduce its headcount. Rumor has it that thousands of people will be offered this incentive to quit or take an early retirement.

Average Age. The second metric in the Human Capital Analytic is the average age of the workforce. Age is not a measure of competence. It is, instead, a measure that can help you predict when some of your most experienced and perhaps skilled people will be walking out the door. This measure is currently very important in the military and many other federal government organizations, because a large percentage of the workforce will be retiring in the next 7 to 10 years. This is predicted to create a huge skill gap until younger people in these organizations can improve their knowledge and skills.

Knowledge/Skills. The hard part of any Human Capital Analytic is the measure of the competence of your people. This metric can range from fairly simple and straightforward to something very sophisticated and complicated. We will look at a very simple measure and then go on to describe more advanced versions.

The Army Corps of Engineers is a huge project planning and management organization consisting of people with a wide variety of technical skills and abilities. Years ago, the Corps came up with an early retirement package that enticed many of its senior people to retire a few years earlier than they had planned. Most of the people who were given the offer took it, and they all walked out the doors in a short period of time. The Corps' bean counters were delighted because payroll costs went down considerably. However, the Corps was having trouble with its projects because a lot of knowledge and experience was now gone. What was needed was a measure of the knowledge and skills of the staff, to quantify the loss that could occur with a number of senior people leaving at one time.

The Sacramento Division of the Corps is one of the pioneers in adopting a balanced scorecard approach to performance metrics. It recently decided to build the new human capital metric around an existing system called METL, an acronym that stands for Mission Essential Task List. Each job description includes a list of competencies and skill requirements (the METLs). Each individual is then assessed on an annual basis to determine what percentage of the METLs he or she possesses. METL scores for the entire division are then aggregated into one overall number that can be broken down by department, job level, or types of knowledge/skills. A person can increase his or her METL score through training and successfully completing job assignments like projects. The overall human capital score moves to the right with the acquisition of new people or skills, and moves to the left when someone leaves the division or the Corps. This is a crude metric, but it is a good start. The Sacramento Division plans to migrate toward a more systematic approach over the next few years as it becomes more adept at performance measurement.

Another client has a more sophisticated and complicated approach. Technical and nontechnical knowledge/skill requirements are listed for each job, along with the level of competency required on a 1 to 7 scale. A rating of 1 indicates a need for rudimentary knowledge. A rating of 7 indicates that a high level of skill mastery is required for the job. Under this rating system, a truck driver might need a level 1 knowledge of the theory of combustion engine operation, but the driver needs a level 7 in driving and navigation skills. Each individual rates his or her own skill level, which is also rated by a supervisor. If the person demonstrates the skill level (or higher), he or she receives a score of 100 percent. Each job is also given a weight from 1 to 10, depending on its level and importance to the company's mission. This human capital metric is quite sophisticated and does take into account that there are vast differences in the skill levels of 10 people who all do the same job.

An R&D organization I worked with had an approach similar to the one described for measuring the level of competency of employees. What this R&D organization also measured for its professional staff was the number of star players it had on its team. In almost every profession, there is a pecking order of people who are the most respected talents in a particular field. But figuring out who is the best baseball pitcher is fairly objective and easy; figuring out who is the best scientist is a little more challenging. For the scientific community, the factors that go into the measure of "star power" include presentations at prestigious conferences, publications of books or articles in prestigious journals, citations of one's work by others, outside speaking and consulting assignments, and resumes received from people who want to work under this individual. Within each scientific discipline, the laboratory attempts to achieve a balance of A, B, C, and D players. Some individuals get hired as D players and move up the scale to eventually become A players. Others are content to remain D players for the duration of their careers. The breakdown of the human capital metric for this R&D lab is shown in Figure 6-20.

Quality of New Hires	15%
Employee Competencies	65%
Star Power	20%

Figure 6-20. Example of the Human Capital Analytic in an R&D Organization

Another client adopted a very sophisticated approach to using some of the metrics already mentioned above by assigning a percentage weight for each of four factors below for each staff position:

1. General abilities and intelligence
2. Job specific technical knowledge and skills
3. Nontechnical knowledge and skills
4. Relationships.

The weights for each factor varied quite a bit depending on the job. Each employee was then given a percentage score based on his or her level of competence in each of the four areas. Scores were then multiplied by the weights to determine the human capital score for each individual. A couple of examples are shown in Figure 6-21.

VP – Information Technology		Finance Clerk
1. Intelligence/ability	30%	15%
2. Technical knowledge/skill	15%	50%
3. Nontech. knowledge/skill	30%	25%
4. Relationships	25%	15%

Figure 6-21. Examples of Human Capital Job Dimension Weights

As you can see, the methods of measuring human capital are about as varied as the types of organizations that exist. Sadly, there is no standard way to calculate intellectual assets in an organization. The American Society for Training & Development (ASTD) has been working for more than 20 years to come up with a method for valuing human assets, and it has not been able to get consensus on how to calculate the measure. There are no standard metrics even within similar industries. The good news about this is that the lack of absolute standards gives you complete flexibility in deciding how to measure this important dimension within your own organization.

People Metric #5: Communication Effectiveness

Ask ten employees in any organization to list their biggest gripe about their employer, and five of them will mention communication. This is very frustrating to leaders who often feel that they could not do more to communicate better with employees. Employee and leadership perceptions on this issue are clearly quite different.

Recently, I facilitated a planning meeting for a military client. The first part of the meeting was devoted to reviewing performance on last year's goals. The organization had set only three goals, and one of them was to improve communication. The client had spent a lot of time and resources over the year to reach this goal. Below is a list of things the client tried:

- creating an employee website,
- redesigning the newsletter and making it larger,
- initiating quarterly all-hands meetings, and
- having more frequent knowledge-sharing sessions.

The only data the group had to prove that communication had gotten better was activity data. In other words, the group could tell you how many people looked at the website or how many attended the all-hands meetings. However, what it did not have a measure of was whether or not the goal had been achieved. In other words, *no one really knew if communication had actually improved.*

Organizations spend a fortune on communication, and most have no measure of how well they have communicated. The following sections describe how to measure the effectiveness of your communication, which is something every leader should be interested in tracking.

Developing a Communication Effectiveness Analytic

Good communication is not exactly rocket science. There are well-researched rules and guidelines about how to best communicate with people using various media. The problem is, most people in most organizations do not follow the rules of good communication.

I have been in hundreds of meetings where no one beyond the first row of seats in the meeting room could read the slides being presented. I have seen many management reports that have graphs that have so many lines of data on them it is impossible to evaluate trends. And I have read many policies and procedures that are so hard to understand that even employees with Ph.D.s would struggle. The people who were attempting to communicate were clearly not communicating effectively. It is safe to assume that they were also not measuring their communication effectiveness and that they did not even have the tools to do so. Essentially, leaders need a Communication Analytic that tells them two things:

1. Are we consistently following the rules for effective communication?
2. Have we really communicated important information to employees and partners?

Based on these two questions, most communication metrics look like the design shown in Figure 6-22; the following paragraphs describe each of these metrics in a bit more detail.

Approach			Effectiveness	
50%			50%	
Output	Process Quality	Frequency	Perceptions	Comprehension
40%	40%	20%	30%	70%

Figure 6-22. Example of a Communication Analytic

Measuring the Quality of Your Communication Output. The design of the example in Figure 6-22 puts half the weight on leading indicators that look at *how* an organization communicates or its approach to communication. The lagging part of the measure is a measure of how effective the communication has been. In measuring the approach, the first thing that gets assessed is the quality of your communication outputs. The dimensions that are usually evaluated include:

- Completeness
- Reading level
- Clarity
- Aesthetics/composition
- Company standards/formats

Standards need to be developed for the dimensions above for the various types of communication media and materials produced by the organization, including:

- E-mails
- PowerPoint slides
- Websites
- Newsletters
- Reports

One client measures these outputs by taking a sample each month and giving it to its Corporate Communications Department to score. The communication pieces are given a 0–100 percent score based on how well they meet established standards. This data is also used as the basis for training needs analysis. When the organization finds that certain mistakes are common, reminders are provided to alert people to their errors, or training is developed if necessary.

Measuring the Communication Process. Along with measuring the outputs themselves, it is important to measure the communication process as well. Some of the process measures that might be considered include:

- Was an analysis done of the audience prior to developing the communication materials?
- Was the most appropriate type of media used?
- Was the communication presented in a clear and concise fashion?
- Were multiple media used to ensure that all employees heard the message?

- Was the communication piece tested with a sample from the target audience?
- Was the person who did the communicating a skilled communicator?

Measuring the Frequency of Your Communications. The last dimension in the approach metric is a measure of communication frequency. Advertising research tells us that people need to be exposed to a message at least 5 times before they hear it. It also helps if the message is delivered using a variety of media. Based on this information, one client organization has a communication rule it calls "5 by 5." What this means is that for any important communication, this company makes sure it is communicated at least five times to employees using five different media.

A measure of frequency in a Communication Analytic might also be an assessment of timeliness. Employees often hear news about their companies from the media before they hear it from corporate headquarters or supervisors. By the time it comes to the employees, they have heard the same news on the morning television and without the corporate spin. For communication to be effective, it needs to be frequently heard and very timely.

Measuring Perceptions of Your Communication. Now we come to the measure of communication effectiveness. In the example shown in Figure 6-22, two dimensions are measured: perceptions and comprehension. Perceptions or opinions are gathered via survey or focus group to determine how employees feel about the communication that comes from corporate and from other parts of the organization. These surveys or questionnaires might also be used to find out people's communication preferences.

Measuring Comprehension of Your Communications. The metric given the highest weight in the effectiveness measure is an evaluation of whether or not the message was received by the audience. Several clients do anonymous testing of a sample of employees following the communication of important information. For example, if the boss has an all-hands meeting every three months, every 10th attendee who walks out at the end gets handed a test with 4 short-answer questions about the presentation. These employees are told not to put their names on the quizzes, so there is no pressure. What this client discovered was that even though employees attended the meetings and appeared to be paying attention, most could not recall the main points of the presentations a few minutes after they were over. The same organization does Internet pop-up quizzes about things like the employee newsletter and reports.

You are probably thinking that all this sounds like a lot of trouble, and that you don't really need a formal metric that assesses communication. Well, to some extent you are right. It is a lot of trouble, but so is doing budgets and tracking costs, and measuring operational performance and the many other things your organization measures with great precision. What you need to recognize, however, is that most organizations (maybe even yours) spend a lot of money and time on communication, and almost none of these organizations have anything more than anecdotal data on its effectiveness. Even a simple survey on employee perceptions regarding communication is a good start, and not that complicated. A more systematic metric can evolve with time.

Chapter Summary

The human resources or people section of most scorecards is the least evolved and yet one of the most important. Most metrics in this area are either lagging (e.g., the number of accidents or percentage of employee turnover); are too infrequent (e.g., an annual morale survey); or lack integrity (e.g., they measure the number of people sitting in classroom chairs, or the number of ethics codes that have been distributed). The alternative suggested here is that every large organization needs to have five major metrics/analytics in this section of the scorecard:

1. Employee Satisfaction
2. Employee Health and Safety
3. Ethics and Diversity
4. Employee Knowledge/Skills/Competencies
5. Communication

This is the section of the scorecard that is almost completely standard and can be applied to any organization. These five metrics are appropriate for manufacturing companies, service companies, hospitals, schools, government, and military organizations.

What goes into these metrics is up to you. Some of the best ones I have seen start with a blank sheet of paper and people brainstorming ways to measure something. All organizations need to have quantifiable metrics that tell them that their employees are happy, healthy, safe, ethical, skilled, and aware of what is going on. This is the section of the scorecard where "How's it going?" data is likely to be strongly influenced by the level and personality of the people asking. Even Jet Blue executives, who fly on their own planes weekly and talk to employees and customers, need to be reminded that they are not always hearing the complete truth when they ask employees how they like their jobs. Having these metrics in your scorecard will help leaders fine-tune their human resource strategies and eliminate those programs or activities that may not be working.

A construction industry client found its employee satisfaction score dipped down for a couple of months and started doing some things that were likely to improve morale. None of them worked, so the company gathered additional data via focus groups to ask employees what they wanted and why they were not satisfied. What the company learned is that employees wanted more of a say in establishing goals and improvement strategies and more involvement in helping the company get better. Wow, what a shock! Executives thought some T-shirts, more overtime, and pizza was what employees wanted, but only by collecting more data was the company able to learn how to *really* improve employee satisfaction.

The next chapter describes how to create meaningful operational or internal analytics. This is one section of the scorecard where one size does not fit all. Each industry/field tends to have it own unique metrics that are used to evaluate success. The challenge with these types of metrics is not coming up with them, but limiting them to a vital few.

Key Points to Keep in Mind
About People Metrics and Analytics

☐ This is probably the most important yet least sophisticated set of metrics on any organization's scorecards.

☐ The quality and integrity of these metrics has not improved much over the years, in spite of much talk about intellectual capital and knowledge management.

☐ Employee satisfaction or engagement is critical to good job performance and cannot be assessed with an annual survey. The best employee satisfaction metrics are analytics that include a variety of hard and soft sub-metrics.

☐ Employee health and safety are more important today than ever due to escalating health care costs and lawsuits. A health and safety analytic needs to include leading/predictive metrics as well as the typical lost-time accidents.

☐ Everyone is concerned with ethics and diversity today, yet most scorecards do not include measures of these factors unless the organization has already been in serious trouble. Both factors are extremely important today and need to be measured and managed.

☐ The knowledge and skills of employees can make or break an organization. All scorecards need to include an analytic that includes meaningful measures of the real competencies of its people, as opposed to meaningless things that are easy to count like degrees and training hours.

☐ One of the biggest problems in any large organization is communication. Every large organization needs to have a metric that tells it how well it is communicating with its employees and other key stakeholders.

7

Operational Analytics: Key Internal Metrics of Quality, Productivity, Timeliness, and Innovation

Operational Analytics summarize important internal measures of performance that link to customer loyalty and financial results. Operational metrics address your day-to-day work as well as major projects or initiatives. In a strategy map or sequence of metrics, the operational measures tend to drive greater customer loyalty and financial results if you pick the right things to measure and set standards or targets appropriately. There are often hundreds of operational metrics in an organization. The key here is to select the most important ones to include on leaders' scorecards. The metrics selected should be the drivers of business success.

People metrics, customer metrics, and financial metrics are pretty much the same in most organizations, but the section of the scorecard that deals with operational metrics varies from organization to organization, depending on the nature of the work it does. Consequently, this chapter presents a generic "straw-man" Operational Analytic, but it is important to note that this straw-man model is subject to tailoring based on specific organizational needs. The chapter also provides some examples of how Operational Analytics can be constructed to suit the needs of various types of organizations and presents some unique metrics that clients have developed in the last few years. The examples are designed to encourage you to consider possible measures for your own scorecard.

To get you started, Figure 7-1 lists the questions that should be answered by the Operational Analytics you choose for your scorecard. In general, the operational metrics in this section of the scorecard address three major themes or performance dimensions: quality, timeliness, and productivity. A generic Operational Analytic might be designed as shown in Figure 7-2.

Operational Analytics provide answers to the following questions:

- ☐ How are we doing on our major projects?
- ☐ Are we consistently producing and delivering high-quality products and services?
- ☐ Are we being productive with our people and other resources?
- ☐ Are the major performance improvement initiatives we are investing in really working?
- ☐ How are we doing at researching and developing new products or services?

Figure 7-1. Questions Answered by Operational Analytics

Project Management Analytic	Productivity Analytic	Process Analytic	Enterprise Excellence Analytic	R&D Analytic

---

Figure 7-2. Sample Metrics for an Operational Analytic

Depending on the type of organization, the weights of the tier-two metrics in the operational analytic will vary greatly. For example, in the Army Corps of Engineers or at the Norfolk Naval Shipyard, everything is a project, so the project management analytic is heavily weighted and there is no Process Analytic. In contrast, in a typical manufacturing company, the process analytic is assigned a big weight, and lower weighting is given to the Project Management Analytic. If people/labor is less than 10 percent of your organization's cost, you might not want to even put a measure of employee productivity on your scorecard. Instead, you might want to include a measure of the productivity of your equipment or raw materials. The rest of this chapter describes in more detail each of the five metrics of the Operational Analytic.

Operational Metric #1: Project Management Analytic

All organizations spend some amount of their time on special projects, along with their regular day-to-day work. Sometimes projects are the lion's share of your work; at other times, they are just extra work that must be done. Regardless of what percentage of time your organization spends on projects, it is probably worth considering a metric on the scorecard that tells leaders how these projects are going. There are two common approaches for organizations to review project performance.

The first approach is to hold a meeting once a month with all the project managers, and go around the table and ask, "How's it going?" The anecdotal data that is collected can be adequate, but you should remember that individual project managers have a strong incentive to paint a rosy picture of their respective projects, even if a project is in trouble. Any problems brought up are usually attributed to suppliers or other departments. If the projects are small and not critical to the organization's success, the informal "How's it going?" data might be adequate. If the projects are large and have a significant impact on the organization's success, another way of reviewing project performance might be more appropriate.

In the other common approach to project performance review, each project manager brings in a boatload of PowerPoint and Gantt charts to the review meeting. The review process involves looking at 40 to 50 individual charts and spreadsheets, and meeting attendees quickly zone out after an hour or two of this. Moreover, this detailed review is conducted even if all the projects are going well, so the meetings are often a big waste of time. In some ways, the meetings resemble a grade school "show & tell," with each project manager getting up in front of the class and telling everyone how well the project is going. Most often, leaders get the spin version of how the project is going because project managers do not want to look bad in front of their bosses and peers.

Leadership's time is too valuable to spend on such show & tell meetings, especially if the projects being dissected are going well. The projects that should be discussed are the ones that are in trouble.

Thus, the challenge is to come up with meaningful measures that provide an objective assessment of how projects are really going, specifically the kinds of measures that will hone in on problem areas in projects that are not going particularly well. Project management metrics should cut through the smoke screen managers often produce when asked about the status of projects that are in trouble.

Constructing a Project Management Analytic

Every Project Management Analytic I have ever helped a client construct includes three lagging measures of a project's success:

- **Budget:** The first sub-metric is designed to tell the project team whether or not they are staying within budget as they make progress in completing project tasks.
- **Quality of deliverables:** The second sub-metric is a measure of defects or quality problems with the outputs or deliverables that get produced during the course of a project. The quality metric often drills down to a number of lower-level metrics that might be measures of accuracy, completeness, or following prescribed standards.
- **Schedule:** The third sub-metric is a measure of milestones being completed on time. The most common way of measuring schedule is to calculate the percentage of milestones met. This is actually a poor metric because milestones are usually not equal in importance—if you just track whether a milestone was met or not, the metric does not take into account the degree or impact of lateness. In other words, an unimportant milestone that was missed by a day counts the same as a major milestone that was missed by eight weeks.

Aircraft Maintenance Example

One approach that may make this analytic more useful is to establish a weight on budget, quality, and schedule differently for each project. One client that repairs jets for the airlines negotiates on the weights of these three factors with the customer on each job. For example, one airline might decide to put a low weight on budget and is willing to pay the repair company overtime to get its plane back in service quickly. On this project, the repair company might establish a weight of 50 percent on schedule and 25 percent on quality and budget. Another client is having financial trouble and is willing to have the repair company take its time getting the plane fixed, as long as the company does it as cheaply as possible. For this client, the weights might be 60 percent on budget or cost and 20 percent on the remaining factors.

The cool thing about this approach is that it forces the customer to define its priorities up front, and it tells the project team which of the three factors (budget, quality of deliverables, or schedule) is most important. At the end of each project, customers fill out a report card, grading the vendor on how it did on each factor. The grades are then multiplied by the weights to arrive at a total project score. Each project score is then given a weight in the overall analytic based on the dollar value of the project and the dollar value of the account.

Figure 7-3 illustrates how this works. The actual data and weights of the various factors are shown first, followed by a depiction of the data using the software. Reviewers of the performance data might choose to drill down by project (i.e., a particular airplane being repaired) first, and then to the individual factors (i.e., budget, quality, schedule) to find where problems exist. A simpler depiction of the same data, displayed on the leader's desktop, is shown in Figure 7-4.

Project Management Factors for Different Clients and Projects

Plane # 1 40%	Plane # 2 15%	Plane # 3 30%	Plane# 4 15%
Budget 50% × 80 = 40	Budget 50% × 30 = 15	Budget 20% × 100 = 20	Budget 30% × 100 = 30
Quality 10% × 100 = 10	Quality 30% × 80 = 24	Quality 40% × 40 = 16	Quality 40% × 40 = 16
Schedule 40% × 60 = 24	Schedule 20% × 100 =20	Schedule 40% × 60 = 24	Schedule 30% × 80 = 24
Totals 74	59	60	70

Project Management Analytic Calculation

74 × 40% = 29.6	59 × 15% = 8.85	60 × 30% = 18	70 × 15% = 10.5

29.6+ 8.85 + 18 + 10.5 = 67/100 = Yellow (Green = 80 or above)

Figure 7-3. Example of How an Airplane Repair Company Weighs

Project Management Analytic		
67/100		

Plane # 1	Plane # 2	Plane # 3	Plane # 4
74/100	59/100	60/100	70/100

Budget	Quality	Schedule
30	80	100

Figure 7-4. Example of Overview of the Aircraft Repair Company's Project Management Analytic

As you can see in Figure 7-4, overall performance is at 67, which puts the analytic in the yellow zone. In this case, none of the projects are showing red or poor performance overall, but there are some red or problem levels depicted on the tier-three metrics. In this example, you can see that for Plane # 2, quality and schedule performance are both solid green, but the project must be way over budget to receive a score of 30 percent. This is bringing the overall score for the project down in the Project Management Analytic because budget is given an importance weight of 50 percent.

Process and Churn: Two Additional Metrics to Consider in a Project Management Analytic

The problem with measuring only budget, quality, and schedule to evaluate the success and progress on a project is that they are all *lagging* metrics. In other words, you have to have already gone over budget or missed the deadline or had some defect for data to be recorded. All three are measures of the past. Therefore, it is wise to include at least one leading indicator in the Project Management Analytic. A few examples from client case files illustrate how this can be done.

Measuring Process. The Sacramento District of the Army Corps of Engineers (ACOE) put a lot of thought into the Project Management Analytic it developed for its new scorecard because the analytic represented most of the work being done. One thing that concerned the ACOE about the district was that project managers often did not plan and manage their projects systematically. Part of the reason for this was that the staff had a great deal of experience and was more comfortable just "winging it." A dimension the ACOE wanted to include in the analytic was a measure of the degree to which a systematic process was followed. In addition, the ACOE felt that the process sub-metric would always be given a weight of 30 percent, so that even if the budget, quality, and schedule showed perfect performance, the overall score for the project would be in the yellow zone.

The process sub-metric was derived from a checklist of activities that should be done on all projects:

- Involving the customer in creating the project plan,
- Holding weekly project review meetings,
- Entering progress data on a weekly basis using the ACOE project management software,
- Inviting key contractors/partners to project review meetings early on, and
- Keeping the project plan up to date as changes occur.

Measuring Churn. Two other clients (Northrop Grumman Newport News Shipbuilding and U.S. Navy Aircraft Carrier Maintenance Team One) came up with another leading indicator that they now include in their Project Management Analytic: churn. *Churn* is defined as changes to key project parameters (such as scope, deliverables, budget, and schedule). What both organizations had found through research is that poor project planning led to excessive churn, which led to poor performance on project outcomes like cost and schedule. Hence, churn was a good leading metric to include in the analytic.

Some amount of churn is normal and expected because it is impossible to estimate all the work that will be needed to maintain a vessel as big as an aircraft carrier. However, experienced project managers were able to define reasonable red, yellow, and green ranges for churn, based on past projects. This was also a measure that was easy to track because every time there was a change to a project, the information had to be updated in the project planning records.

Another example that illustrates the churn metric on a smaller scale involves a neighbor of mine who had his house torn down a year ago and is building a new one on the same lot. The move-in date has been changed many times, and the scope of the project has changed as well. Some of the changes were a result of alterations requested by the neighbor, but others were caused by the contractor's poor planning, poor-quality work, or failure to meet building codes. The churn metric on this construction project would clearly be in the red zone. If my neighbor had a process metric, that would probably be red as well.

Benefits of Measuring Process and Churn. By making process or churn part of your Project Management Analytic, you will have a more balanced measure of project performance. To roll each individual project up into the overall performance metric, you need to decide which projects get counted and roll up the boss's scorecard. One client measures only the top five most important and costly projects each year in his Project Management Analytic. In contrast, the Norfolk Naval Shipyard counts all projects, but it assigns them a weight based on their size (measured in labor-days) and importance to the Navy. This way, the major dollar projects and other important projects do much more to drive the overall Project Management Analytic than do the smaller ones. However, the CO still wants to know if a small project is in trouble, so even though a small one might not move the overall analytic into the yellow or red, it would certainly turn the little warning light on the analytic red. This is the cue for the CO to drill down into project-level data to locate which one is showing poor performance.

Operational Metric #2: Productivity Analytic

The purpose of this measure on the scorecard is to tell leaders and managers if their expensive resources are being productive. Productivity usually links directly to profitability. It is important to remember, however, that a balanced scorecard includes more than one metric. Like any other measure of performance, productivity is important, but it needs to be tempered with other performance measures. The example below illustrates this critical point.

In the 1970s, productivity was the fad du jour. Companies put productivity in the spotlight, and it got better: People worked harder, equipment worked longer hours, and companies got more use out of their raw materials. However, this demand for greater productivity caused problems with morale, safety, and most often, quality. Remember American cars in the 1970s? GM was cranking out a lot of cars per day, but the quality was bad, and morale at GM (and in the auto industry at large) was quite low. Some workers were letting management know how unhappy they were in peculiar ways: I remember hearing stories of beer bottles being left inside newly assembled car doors. In this and other ways, the productivity boom was being severely damaged by a performance and morale bust. As this example shows, a good Productivity Analytic cannot be limited to a single metric.

Measuring Employee Productivity

For many organizations today, payroll is the single biggest expense. Benefit and pension costs keep rising, along with salaries and wages, so it is important to measure what these costs are paying for. Most people I know work their tails off these days. Moreover, while technology has increased real productivity in a number of industries, this is not necessarily the case in most white-collar jobs. Few managers have the luxury of taking leisurely lunches or going home at 5:00. It is difficult to gauge whether today's managers are being more productive, as productive, or less productive than their counterparts of days gone by, who did have the time to take those lunches and head home at a reasonable hour. One of the reasons for this difficulty is that knowledge work is hard to quantify and measure. One meaningful measure of employee productivity is the "Employee Distraction Analytic." This metric is not only important (it links to wasted dollars), it is also simple to use and easy to track and does not require any extra staff or software. It tells managers how much time is being spent by their people doing what they were actually hired to do and, conversely, how frequently and to what extent they are being distracted from doing what they should be doing.

The bigger the organization, the more distractions tend to exist. People are stressed out and working 60 hours a week, but only 20 hours are actual productive work. The problem is not caused by lazy people; the real culprit is the organization itself! It was, after all, the organization that invented or purchased things that distract people and the organization that told people how important these things are.

The way data is collected for this analytic is to have all employees fill out a daily or weekly time sheet, sorting their time into three categories:

1. **Job tasks:** Doing what you were hired to do (e.g., sales, engineering, accounting, etc.)
2. **Administrative tasks:** Doing tasks that employees in all large organizations have to deal with (attending budget meetings, attending sexual harassment training, learning new e-mail system, etc.)
3. **Programs:** Handling management and other types of programs and processes designed to improve performance (e.g., CRM, ABC, Six Sigma, technical training, Lean, Knowledge Management, or whatever management fads your organization is currently enamored with).

The client that came up with this metric was Discover Financial Services. Anecdotal data told this company that it had too many initiatives and programs going on that were distracting people from doing their jobs. No one had any data on this, but there was a consensus that it was too much. To see how bad it really was, and to gather evidence that could be used to start cutting back on some of these distractions, the company came up with this idea. The distraction metric was initially considered as something the company would put on the scorecard for a few years until it got a handle on the distraction problem. But because distractions have a nasty habit of creeping back in if they are not monitored, the company decided to leave it on its scorecard. Eight years later, the metric is still on the company's scorecard.

In the intervening years, many client organizations (manufacturing companies, service companies, military organizations, universities, and government departments) have put some version of the Distraction Analytic on their scorecards. They have discovered that employees actually like this metric, because distractions are a great source of frustration and the metric is doing something to *reduce* the distractions. On the other hand, distraction reduction can be a two-edged sword: Some people will fight very hard against cutting back or eliminating programs or requirement that they are responsible for implementing.

When you collect baseline data on this metric, you are likely to be unpleasantly surprised with the amount of time people spend doing category 2 and 3 work, or in other words, being distracted from doing their real jobs. Some organizations keep the data collection simple and limit the time coding to the three categories mentioned above (job tasks, administrative tasks, programs). They also tell employees to record only chunks of time of an hour or more. Other clients want to be able to slice and dice the data into individual distractions to find out how much time each task or effort is really taking. Not only do employees have to record that they spent 12 hours this week on category 3 tasks (programs), but they have to code the time, for example, as 1.5 hours spent on Six Sigma team meeting, 6 hours on CRM data entry, 2 hours on time management program, and 2.5 hours on process documentation. This makes the coding system more cumbersome for employees, but having this level of detail is very useful because it clearly shows which activities are taking too much time.

Getting people to be disciplined enough to record their time in this manner depends on the culture of your organization. Lawyers, accountants, and some consultants are accustomed to tracking their time in 15-minute intervals and keep excellent records, so a system like this is easy to implement in law offices, accounting firms, and consulting companies. But in a software design firm where no one has ever even done a time sheet, getting a bunch of creative knowledge workers to track their time this way will be a tough sell. In such cases, it is best to make the data collection simple at first. You can gradually introduce more detailed timekeeping once people get used to it. What will motivate them to keep doing it is seeing the organization start cutting back on some of the distractions so they can spend more time doing their jobs.

Measuring Productivity of Your Other Resources

If it is possible to measure real employee productivity like outputs per hour or something similar, you might include these as sub-metrics in your productivity measure. You might even include a measure of the productivity of your major assets, like equipment or real estate. Many businesses already do this. Almost all hotels have "Rev-PAR" on their scorecards (revenue per available room). Most airlines track RASM and CASM on their scorecards (Revenue per Available Seat Mile and Cost per Available Seat Mile). Retail stores all measure sales per square foot as a productivity measure. The factors that go into your Productivity Analytic will vary, depending on the type of business you are in.

Figures 7-5 and 7-6 show a couple of examples. The airline in Figure 7-5 decided to measure the overall productivity of its line employees: ticket agents, pilots, and maintenance personnel. It also wanted a productivity metric for office workers and people employed in the corporate office and chose to use the Distraction Analytic to measure this. The third metric in the airline Productivity Analytic is one that looks at the productivity of the aircraft. You can see this is broken down into RASM, CASM, Yield, and Load.

Figure 7-6 is an example of a manufacturing organization, where the biggest costs are often equipment, energy, and raw materials. Employee productivity is measured, but it is given a low weight because the production process is highly automated. The manufacturing example is probably the easier one to understand and use because it is easy to measure the outputs. The figure does not show the distraction metric, but it could be included as well to cover salaried employees, who tend to be distracted more than hourly employees.

Employee Analytic	Distraction Analytic	Aircraft Analytic	
20%	15%	65%	
RASM*	CASM**	Yield	Load
25%	25%	25%	25%

*RASM = revenue per available seat mile
**CASM = cost per available seat mile

Figure 7-5. Example of a Productivity Analytic for an Airline

Equipment	Energy	Employee	Raw Material
40%	25%	15%	20%

Figure 7-6. Example of a Productivity Analytic for a Manufacturing Company

Operational Metric #3: Process Analytic

All organizations have two major types of processes:

- those involved in producing the organization's goods or service, and
- support or administrative processes.

Both types of processes obviously add value, or you wouldn't be doing them. In fact, the term "value-added" has become a popular buzzword and has been used by the Baldrige Award criteria to describe those activities that are the factory or direct labor processes. In a restaurant, value-added processes would be food buying, food preparation, serving, bussing, dishwashing, etc. In a hospital, some of the value-added processes would be surgery, lab work, admitting, food services, cleaning, patient care/treatment, diagnosis, etc.

The purpose of the Process Analytic is to tell managers how well the organization is performing the key work processes that link to its mission or reasons for existence. Financial results are often an outcome of well-performed value-added processes, but these measures more directly focus on how well the work is being done. At the executive level, the measure is a summary of all major value-added processes. As you look at scorecards for lower-level managers, the focus is only on the processes they own or play a part in performing.

Creating a Process Analytic

With any work process, there are four points at which to collect data:

1. **Inputs.** Inputs to a process might include raw materials, information, specifications or standards, training/knowledge, references, tools and equipment, and people.
2. **Process.** These are measures that occur as the work is being performed. They may be measures of employee behavior, or they may be technical dimensions. For example, two process measures for the baking process are time and temperature. Process measures must occur during the work process and are leading indicators of key outcome metrics that link to customer requirements: For

an airline, the average speed of a plane (which is a process measure that occurs during the work process) links to an on-time landing (which is a customer requirement).

3. **Outputs.** All work processes are designed to produce some outcome. The outcomes might be a physical product, such as drywall installed, a report or some kind of paper outcome, or an accomplishment, like a correctly repaired car. Outcomes are often fairly easy to inspect and measure. However, these are *lagging* indicators.

4. **Outcomes.** Outcomes are good or bad things that result from the outputs. For example, a well-built house done on time might lead to a happy customer and referrals. Similarly, an order being delivered accurately and on time might lead to future orders. In contrast, a car that was not fixed right the first time might lead to a customer taking his car elsewhere next time (lost business). Outcomes are also lagging indicators, but they tend to be things that the organization places high value on like sales, profits, reputation, and loyal customers.

Typical weighting of these four factors in a Process Analytic is shown in Figure 7-7. As you can see, the weights are well balanced: 50 percent of the metric are leading indicators (Inputs and Processes) and 50 percent are lagging or past-focused indicators.

Inputs	20%
Process	30%
Outputs	30%
Outcomes	20%

Figure 7-7. Typical Weighting for the 4 Sub-Metrics of a Process Analytic

Product/Service Quality Analytic

Some organizations today are obsessed with looking at everything in terms of their key processes. Johnson & Johnson, for example, even designed its scorecard architecture around its major business processes. Another approach, typically used by organizations with executives who are more concerned with product and service quality (hospitals, e.g.) is to put a high-level analytic on the scorecard that looks at quality metrics. A hospital might develop a Quality Analytic like the one in Figure 7-8.

Clinical Quality Standards	Patient Care Standards	Internal Service Standards
45%	35%	20%

Figure 7-8. Example of a Quality Analytic for a Hospital

For an example of a Service Quality Analytic, consider the Work-force Development Division (WDD) in the City of Los Angeles, which helps find adults and youth jobs, gets out-of-school youths back into school, and helps employers fill jobs with good people. WDD is one of the pioneer departments in the city to adopt the analytics approach to performance measurement. It has six categories of data on its score-card, corresponding to the six results categories in the Baldrige model. One of the six categories includes hard objective measure of how WDD does at finding people good jobs and educational opportunities, and finding employees good people to fill their open positions. The Service Quality Analytic that WDD came up with is shown in Figure 7-9. The numbering system is intended to show the hierarchical rela-tionships between the various metrics.

Operational Metric #4: Enterprise Excellence

Most large organizations today are embarking on or in the middle of a number of initiatives designed to save money and improve perfor-mance—for example, CRM, which was discussed in Chapter 6. This section of the current chapter describes how to construct an analytic that tells executives whether or not they are really making good progress with initiatives such as the following:

- Six Sigma
- Lean

1.1 People 70%			1.2 Organizations 30%	
1.1.1 Adults	**1.1.2 Youth**	**1.1.3 OSY***	**1.2.1 Jobs**	**1.2.2 Business Services**
50%	**25%**	**25%**	**75%**	**25%**
1.1.1.1 Placement 40%	1.1.2.1 Credentials 35%	1.1.3.1 Placement 35%	1.2.1.1 % Hired 50%	1.2.2.1 Engagements 40%
1.1.1.2 Wage Gain 20%	1.1.2.2 Ed. Placement 30%	1.1.3.2 Ed. Placement 20%	1.2.1.2 Retention 25%	1.2.2.2 Breadth 10%
1.1.1.3 Retention 30%	1.1.2.3 Job Placement 20%	1.1.3.3 Enroll/Pop. 20%	1.2.1.3 Demand Occ. 25%	1.2.2.3 Org. Quality Placement 50%
1.1.1.4 Credentials 10%	1.1.2.4 Retention 20%	1.1.3.4 Credentials 15%	1.1.3.5 Retention 15%	

Figure 7-9. 1.0 Service Quality Analytic for The Los Angeles Workforce Development Division

- Knowledge management
- Activity-based costing/management
- ISO (International Standards Organization) Certification
- Balanced scorecard
- Joint commission,
- Baldrige

With any of these initiatives, it is important to have some quantifiable measures of their success besides anticipated cost savings that seldom really materialize. Some organizations have had great success with the initiatives listed above. Others, however, have spent a lot of money and time and not really achieved anything notable. The key is to learn this before it is too late, and if the initiative is not working, to find out why.

Organizations are often engaged in a wide variety of ongoing programs and initiatives that are generally accepted as worthwhile and valuable. Your safety program, sales training program, or employee team-building efforts might all be things you have been doing for years and are good examples of this. Even though you don't have quantifiable data on their effectiveness, evidence of their value exists: People are happy with the way they are working, and they don't need to have statistics to prove it. Because of this evidence, there is no need to include these types of programs in your Enterprise Excellence Analytic.

What should be included in this measure are *new* initiatives and programs that will cost your organization a lot of money and time and are of real interest to top management. The initiatives that go into this metric do not have to be limited to management programs with 3-letter acronyms. Along these lines, one client put a metric in the Enterprise Excellence Analytic that addressed the implementation of Peoplesoft. Another put a metric in the analytic that measured the success of a multimillion-dollar software package it bought from EDS to improve its transaction-process operations.

Constructing an Enterprise Excellence Analytic

Your first task is to identify the initiatives that currently are being implemented in your organization and establish a weight for each one, depending on its importance and the resources needed for implementation. Figure 7-10 illustrates how one aerospace organization set weights for two major initiatives and two minor initiatives it had implemented.

Lean Sigma	Activity-Based Management	Knowledge Management	ISO
35%	15%	30%	20%

Figure 7-10. Example of an Enterprise Excellence Analytic for an Aerospace Company

Activity-Based Management and ISO were initiatives that had been going on for several years, and the company was in a maintenance mode with these programs. In contrast, however, major resources were being dumped into the newly implemented Lean Sigma (a combination of Lean and Six Sigma) and Knowledge Management, so it was important to put a high weight on those. The latter two initiatives were also deemed important because they were of interest to senior management, which viewed them from the perspective of potential bottom-line payoff.

In another case, a hospital wanted to have a metric on the CEO's scorecard that would tell him how well the various initiatives were going. The hospital had a vision of winning a Baldrige Award and achieving Nursing Magnet status, and it was also working to maintain Joint Commission certification, which is now done by surprise audit. There was a great deal of overlap in the standards and results assessed in all three of these initiatives, but the CEO wanted to look at them separately and collectively, so this was the perfect type of situation where an analytic metric makes sense.

The Enterprise Excellence Analytic we constructed for this hospital looked like the one presented in Figure 7-11. The process of getting the organization aligned with the Baldrige criteria is given the most weight because the Baldrige model is very comprehensive and covers all hospital processes and results. Improving alignment with Baldrige will also help meet the standards for the Joint Commission and Nursing Magnet.

Joint Commission	Baldrige	Nursing Magnet
25%	50%	25%

Figure 7-11. An Example of an Enterprise Excellence Analytic for a Hospital

Once you have identified the improvement initiatives and assigned a weight to each one based on its importance to your organization, the next task is to figure out how to measure whether the programs are successful. As with any process, there are four categories of metrics that should go into the Enterprise Excellence Analytic: Inputs, Processes, Outputs, and Outcomes. Some examples of each of these four types of measures for currently popular improvement initiatives are shown in Figures 7-12 and 7-14.

Knowledge Management Metrics. A big challenge for many organizations today is to document and pass on important knowledge to others, so they can benefit from past discoveries. This was a challenge even centuries ago, one that led to the invention of books. Books still remain the predominant way that most knowledge is documented and passed on to others. Today, however, we also have electronic databases that provide us with online access to books, papers, research, videos, and even diagnostics. In spite of this wealth of easily accessible data from a variety of sources, very little has been done to measure how much and how well it serves any given organization.

In a study done by the American Productivity and Quality Center, many companies that are implementing Knowledge Management (KM) systems have no way to measures their effectiveness. They point to traditional lagging measures like growth and profits, but it would be a real stretch to suggest that a company's growth is mostly due to its Knowledge Management program. Therefore, organizations that are spending thousands or even millions on KM need to have a metric on executives' scorecards that tell them whether or not the program is adding value. "How's it going?" data is not sufficient for any effort this large and expensive. Instead, an effective Knowledge Management Analytic should be composed of four types of data, with examples for each, as shown in Figure 7-12.

In constructing a KM Analytic, a company just getting started with the program should consider putting 70 or more percent of the weight on the input and process measures, because the outputs and outcomes will be few or none in the initial year or two. As the company begins to more fully deploy a comprehensive KM system, the weights of the individual metrics in the analytic should evolve to focus more on outcomes and outputs. The example shown in Figure 7-13 depicts the changing weights of the individual sub-metrics.

A Navy client searched for the best practices when it came to KM metrics and found that most of the activity measures that various companies tracked did not correlate to any meaningful outcomes. These companies were counting number of databases that were built, website hits on those databases, presentations made, and knowledge-sharing meetings held. There was lots of activity, but no real evidence that any of these things improved performance in the company. The

1. **Awareness or Input Measures** (examples)
   - Employee awareness of what types of knowledge need to be documented
   - KM tools and system
   - Benchmarking data from KM systems in other companies
   - Forms and processes for documenting knowledge

2. **Behavior or Process Measures** (examples)
   - Attendance at KM training
   - Participation in KM activities such as committees/teams
   - Making presentations
   - Leading knowledge-sharing sessions
   - Creating KM databases
   - Documenting knowledge
   - Researching best practices
   - Building a KM website or database

3. **Output Measures**—these include measures of the quality, accuracy, completeness, and timeliness of KM outputs, such as:
   - Best practices documentation
   - Decision-making aids
   - White papers
   - Presentations
   - Training materials

4. **Outcome Measures** (examples)
   - Adoption of best practices by others
   - Awards and recognition for KM system
   - The impact of new knowledge on key outcome measures or organizational performance, such as new product sales, productivity, growth, profits, cost reduction, or quality improvement

Figure 7-12. Sample Measures to Consider for a
Knowledge Management Analytic

KM metric this client was most impressed with was the approach being used by Ford Motor Company.

Ford's approach was to measure only outputs and outcomes. The company had been down the road of measuring activity, and it found

KM Analytic	Year 1	Year 3	Year 5
Inputs	30%	20%	10%
Process	40%	30%	20%
Outputs	20%	30%	40%
Outcomes	10%	20%	30%

Figure 7-13. Example of How the Weight of Various Knowledge
Management Analytics Should Change Over Time

that all this did was reward people for what could be wasteful effort. Instead, what Ford measures for its KM program is how many ideas were developed in one part of the company that were then *adopted* and *implemented* in other parts of the company. Ford also measured how the implementation of these approaches and ideas paid off in bottom-line outcome measures.

Navy Carrier Team One loved the Ford approach, but it was concerned with a metric that was strictly rear-view mirror—i.e., lagging. This became an even bigger concern because NCTO, which was just getting started with KM, realized that it would take a while for outcomes to materialize. To alleviate these concerns, NCTO came up with a KM Analytic that is shown in Figure 7-14. You can see that the KM Vitality Index (or analytic) is made up of two tier-two metrics: KSN Commitment (40 percent) and Proven Practice Replication (60 percent). The Proven Practice Replication metric is the lagging measure that NCTO derived from Ford's metric. The KSN (Knowledge-Sharing Network) Commitment metric is the leading indicator of activity, which looks at how engaged various parts of the organization are in knowledge management practices. For example, a low level of engagement indicates an organization that sends a few low-level people to the Knowledge-Sharing meetings, individuals who rarely contribute anything or complete any assignments given to them. On the other hand, a high level of engagement is shown when an organization not only has a large number of high-level talented individuals participate, but also chooses to involve people who are actively engaged in leadership roles and complete important assignments.

```
┌─────────────────────────────────────────────────────────┐
│            Knowledge-Sharing Network Vitality Analytic     │
│      KSN Commitment              Proven Practice Replication │
│          40%                            60%                │
│          ├──────────────────────────────────┤            │
│      Participation                    Engagement          │
│          25%                            75%                │
└─────────────────────────────────────────────────────────┘
```

Figure 7-14. Example of a Knowledge Management Analytic
for Navy Carrier Team One

Lean or Six Sigma Metrics. Both Lean and Six Sigma have helped many organizations improve the efficiency of their work processes. Building a metric or analytic that tells senior management how well the programs are working is very similar to the approach described for creating a Knowledge Management metric. An analytic for any performance improvement initiative needs to include the four basic categories of metrics already mentioned: input, process, output, and outcomes. A Six Sigma or Lean Analytic should also evolve with time as your organization more fully deploys the program. Early on, the weight on the sub-metrics should be on inputs and process; later, it should evolve toward a greater focus on outputs and outcomes. Some possible metrics to consider in each category are shown in Figure 7-15.

Six Sigma and Lean should both have a positive effect on many scorecard metrics in an organization. The test of whether you are measuring the right things in your Lean or Six Sigma analytic is the link to other scorecard metrics. If the Lean gauge is always green and the key measures of company performance like productivity and profitability are consistently red, you probably have the wrong metrics in your Lean/Six Sigma Analytic. This metric ought to be a leading indicator or predictor of many measures of organizational success, but it is by no means to be viewed as the only indicator. If company profits increase, you can't just point to your Six Sigma effort as the major reason for that increase.

This same sort of breakdown of four types of metrics can be used for an initiative such as a major new software program, leadership development program, or any other initiative that costs a lot of money and is supposed to improve organizational performance.

1. **Input Metrics** (examples)
   - # of people trained and the level of training (e.g., green belt, black belt, etc.), processes identified for study/improvement
   - # of teams formed
   - Direction/goals from senior management
   - Resources received
   - Process documentation
   - Performance data

2. **Process Metrics** (examples)
   - # of teams formed
   - Team meetings held
   - Level of engagement of team members
   - Processes documented
   - Benchmarking studies completed
   - Processes analyzed using the proper approach
   - Research/studies conducted using proper methods
   - Use of systematic processes while doing projects
   - Proper documentation of progress
   - Involvement of process stakeholders/owners
   - Knowledge-sharing activities with other organizations

3. **Output Metrics** (examples)
   - # of process maps created
   - Research study quality and thoroughness
   - Integrity of process data
   - Sufficient trend data collected
   - Thoroughness of analyses completed
   - Milestones completed on time
   - Budget performance on improvement projects
   - Stakeholder feedback
   - Presentations made
   - Clarity and thoroughness of documentation on improved processes
   - Linkages of Six Sigma/Lean initiatives to company goals/objectives

(continued on next page)

Figure 7-15. Sample Measures to Consider for a
Lean or Six Sigma Analytic

---

4. Outcome Metrics (examples)

- Cost reductions
- Cycle time improvements
- Improvements in safety
- Waste/scrap reduction
- Quality or yield improvement
- Improved margins or profits
- Increases in employee satisfaction
- Awards or recognition for team projects
- Increased resources for Lean or Six Sigma efforts
- Deployment of Lean or Six Sigma in daily operation of the organization
- Increased support of effort by employees and management

Figure 7-15. (*Continued*)

Operational Metric #5: Research and Development

Research and Development (R&D) functions are not limited to manufacturing organizations: All types of service and nonprofit organizations develop and introduce new products and services. In companies like Bose and Medtronic, R&D is a real competitive edge. Bose spends about twice what any of its competitors spend on R&D. The payoff is that Bose is usually first in the marketplace with some new audio product that consumers love. Sales of new products are a great metric for R&D, but often many years of research, development, and testing are required before a product is released in the marketplace. The challenge is to measure whether or not R&D is working on the right stuff.

Another challenge is not to destroy the creativity of your people by setting goals, having review meetings, and implementing a structured set of metrics for R&D. For example, many a great band's creativity has been lost after signing a record deal and agreeing to a new album each year. The band cranks out a new record each year, but few of these are any good. Setting goals and measuring progress on creative work is tricky. One alternative is to hire a bunch of really smart people and leave them alone until they come up with something cool that you think will sell. Most organizations are not willing to take such a radical approach, recognizing that even a creative process like research and development needs to be measured in some ways.

The R&D Function as a System

Just like any work process, research and development is a system that consists of inputs, processes, outputs, and outcomes. Figure 7-16 lists some of the measures you might consider when developing an R&D

1. **Inputs.** The major inputs to the R&D process are:
   - market research,
   - customer feedback,
   - competitor data,
   - information on new technologies or findings, tools, equipments and resources, goals, and information on company direction
   - Other inputs for R&D might be problems or specific requests from marketing, engineering, manufacturing, and other departments.

2. **Processes.** There are a number of processes that go in an R&D function:
   - writing proposals,
   - making presentations,
   - attending meetings,
   - conducting research,
   - developing prototypes,
   - testing and evaluation,
   - documenting findings,
   - preparing publications,
   - developing project plans,
   - communicating/deploying new technologies, and
   - obtaining funding.

3. **Outputs.** R&D produces a number of outputs that can be measured, including:
   - patents,
   - papers,
   - publications,

(continued on next page)

Figure 7-16. Sample Measures to Consider for an R&D Metric

---

3. **Outputs.** (*continued*)

- prototypes,
- study results/data,
- project plans,
- grant applications,
- proposals,
- new products,
- new knowledge or technologies.

4. **Outcomes.** The receiving systems for R&D's outputs are marketing, business planning, manufacturing, engineering, distributors, and end customers. Some of the major outcomes that results from R&D's processes and outputs include:

- $ in new product sales,
- profits from new product sales,
- cost reductions,
- cycle time reductions,
- improved product performance,
- capital avoidance,
- improvements in market share,
- attraction of new customers, and
- greater loyalty from existing customers.

Figure 7-16. (*Continued*)

metric, and Figure 7-17 is a systems model of an R&D function, with measurement points identified. Finally, Figure 7-18 shows what a good R&D Analytic for the CEO's scorecard might look like.

Case Study: Momentum Textiles' R&D

Momentum Textiles is a textile design and manufacturing firm in Irvine, California. An industry leader, Momentum designs fabrics for the furniture and architectural and design community. The company's fabrics are used in hotels, restaurants, and other commercial environments. Momentum does not have an R&D function in the same sense as a company like Bose, but it does have a process called "Design," which is really a new-product-development function.

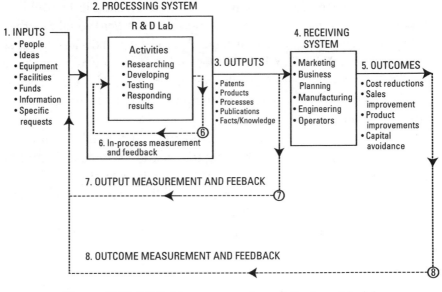

Figure 7-17. R&D Measurements and System Model

Input	Process Metrics	Output	Outcomes
20%	15%	30%	35%

Figure 7-18. Sample Weightings of Sub-Metrics for an R&D Analytic

Momentum's R&D Input Metrics. The input metrics that go into the Design Analytic for Momentum are the quality and thoroughness of the information it gathers on fashion trends, furniture trends, and other market information. The designers who are most in touch with the customer industries they serve tend to design fabrics clients really like and end up buying.

Momentum's R&D Process Metrics. The company's design process metrics focus on:

- how much time the designers spend with customers,
- cycle time for new designs, and
- testing new designs with customers.

Over the years, Momentum has learned a valuable lesson: The fabrics that customers say they like the most are *not* the fabrics they ended up buying. Company reps have also discovered that asking customers which fabrics they like the best is not a good way to evaluate new designs. Momentum still asks customers to evaluate fabric samples, but company reps now record customer *behavior* rather than customer comments.

What Momentum looks for and records is which fabric sample a customer picks up first and how long the customer holds it. Company research and company reps confirm that the fabrics that get picked up first and held the longest are the ones that sell, not the ones customers say they like. After documenting this information for groups of customers, Momentum discovered it had a great process metric—one that correlates to sales of new fabrics.

To facilitate and enhance designer contact with customers, each designer was assigned to an industry sales group and now works full-time for a particular industry. That is, one designer works with the hotel and restaurant business, another works in healthcare, and another works in the commercial office furniture industry.

Momentum's R&D Output Metrics. Output metrics include:

- the number of new fabrics that are designed,
- the number of home runs (big sellers) versus strike outs, and
- the cost of the new designs, as well as cycle time.

Momentum's R&D Outcome Measures. Outcome measures are:

- design cost divided by total company gross margin and sales,
- company revenue from new products, and
- design awards.

The Importance of Fast Design Cycle Time to R&D

About ten years ago, I was working with Ericsson's cell phone business. Ericsson had a very thorough new product development and testing process, which ensured that when a product was released, it was good quality. The problem was that all this thoroughness took too long. By the time Ericsson came out with a new phone, it was old news—Nokia already had taken a similar phone to market eight months earlier. It took Ericsson twice as long as it took Nokia to research and develop the new product. Today, one company is a household name; the other is not. The competitive edge often goes to the company with the best cycle time. Companies that can develop and introduce new products fastest often capture the lion's share of the market before tastes change.

Not surprisingly, cycle time for many products has accelerated. In the past, Nokia developed a new phone in 12 to 18 months; now, the development process takes 6 to 9 months. Similarly, Nissan, which used to take 21 months to develop a new car model, is now releasing new models in only 10 months.

Cycle time is even more important in the fashion businesses. H&M, a very successful Swedish retailer with stores in the United States and Europe, can go from sketch board to rack in just three weeks! Fashion trends develop quickly but also dissipate quickly. If you don't have a hot product on the racks when people want it, they won't wait. In most cases, they will soon be looking for another item (maybe something they saw Paris Hilton wearing it in the latest issue of *Star* magazine).

For a retail clothing company like H&M, an important input metric measures awareness of what is hot. Knowledge of a trend is a key success measure for capitalizing on the latest trend. The timeliness of that information is also critical. By the time most of us get wind of a trend, it is on its way out. A *process metric* identifies the right source for fabric and manufacturing. H&M uses many contract manufacturers, and the company needs to select the right one based on expertise, location, and workload. *Output metrics* measure things like number of units produced, number of units in stores, cycle time for delivery, product quality, and the right quantity shipped to each store to match demands.

Chapter Summary

The operational section of an organization's scorecard should focus on answering these major questions:

1. How are we progressing on our major projects? (This corresponds to the Project Management Analytic.)
2. Are we maximizing the productivity of our people and other resources? (This corresponds to the Productivity Analytic.)
3. Are we consistently meeting our standards for quality products and services? (This corresponds to the Process Analytic.)
4. Are the performance improvement programs or initiatives we are investing in really working? (This corresponds to the Enterprise Excellence Analytic.)
5. How are we doing at coming up with new products and services that meet market needs? (And this corresponds to the R&D Analytic.)

These are the five basic questions that require quantifiable answers. Designing the operational section of your scorecard around these five analytics provides a good balance of past, present, and future. The productivity and quality measures are mostly lagging metrics of the past. The Project Management and Enterprise Excellence Analytics are measures of the present and future, and the R&D Analytic is mostly focused on measures of future performance.

The five analytics recommended for inclusion on this section of your scorecard should be considered a generic starting point. As mentioned at the beginning of this chapter, the operational section of the scorecard is the one that is most subject to customization, based on the nature of an organization. In an organization like the Army Corps of Engineers, the Project Management Analytic is vitally important and represents most of the organization's work; consequently, there may be no need for a measure of product or service quality or research and development, because the organization does not do R&D and has no real products or services. In a manufacturing scorecard, there may be no need for a Project Management Analytic or an Enterprise Excellence Analytic, but there should probably be separate metrics for product quality and service quality.

Feel free to tailor the metrics that go in this section of your score-card as much as necessary to make it suit your needs. But keep the following guidelines in mind:

- There should be no more than six high-level analytics in this section of the scorecard.
- Try to balance past, present, and future time perspectives in your metrics.
- Think about the basic concepts of quality, productivity, timeliness, and innovations as the major dimensions that are usually covered in this section of the scorecard.
- Most of these metrics should relate back to the core mission and products or services of your organization.
- Make sure to include standard industry metrics somewhere in your analytics, even if they are not flawless.

Financial and strategic analytics are covered in the next chapter. Even though there are standard financial metrics used to evaluate an enterprise, different organizations tend to favor different financial metrics. Chapter 8 describes how to select the right financial measures to go into your analytics and how to measure the success of your most important strategies: those most strongly linked to your organization's vision.

Key Points to Keep in Mind
About Operational Metrics and Analytics

☐ Operational metrics provide data on how well the organization is performing its overall mission, as well as on major projects.

☐ All industries and fields have their own unique operational metrics that go in this section of the scorecard.

☐ All organizations have these types of metrics, but most track far too many of them, so analytics provide a great way of combining a number of these individual metrics into summary gauges of overall performance.

☐ Most organizations need to have a metric that tells management about the progress being made on major capital or other types of projects.

☐ Operational metrics tend to focus on quality, productivity, timeliness, process, and innovation.

☐ Researching and developing new products and services may be a process that requires its own analytic in some organizations.

☐ Most large organizations are investing in some sort of improvement initiative such as Lean, Six Sigma, or Activity-Based Costing. Executives need a metric on the scorecard that provides objective data on the success of these initiatives.

8

Strategic and Financial Analytics: Measuring What Really Matters

Strategic measures tell an organization's leaders how it is progressing toward its vision. In most cases, it is helpful to separate the strategic or vision-related measures from those that link to an organization's purpose or mission. There will typically be 10 to 15 mission-related metrics on a scorecard, but there should only be a few that link to the vision. For example, if your vision is growth, then you might include a growth metric in this section of the scorecard, along with measures of your two major growth strategies.

Financial measures on a scorecard provide a *summary* of a few key statistics that tell reviewers how the organization is performing from a financial perspective. The big challenge with financial statistics is narrowing them down to three to four. Another thing to remember is that traditional financial metrics are all focused on the past. Metrics on a balanced scorecard should include some leading indicators.

Like operational metrics, the financial and strategic metrics on your scorecard should be customized to accommodate your vision and the nature of your organization. Although there are some standard financial metrics, such as sales and profits that may end up on score-cards for most businesses, even these may need to be customized for individual preference. Most leaders in business have favorite financial statistics or ratios that they like to watch. Unlike models in other chapters of this book, the generic models in this chapter will probably not match your particular financial and strategic metrics. However, by seeing examples of how other organizations construct this section of the scorecard, you will be able to apply the concepts these models illustrate to your own financial and strategic metrics.

Figure 8-1 lists the questions that should be answered by strategic and financial metrics, in businesses, nonprofit organizations, and government agencies. Strategic measures in all of these organizations tell leaders whether or not progress is being made in achieving the organizational vision. Sometimes, the strategic measures and the financial measures overlap: If your vision is to rank #3 in market share, then market share is a good strategic metric. More often, strategic measures link to specific strategies that are being deployed to achieve a vision: If a school district's vision is to become nationally recognized as one of the best school districts in the United States, it might have a strategic metric that measures its progress in deploying the Baldrige criteria throughout the district.

For a business, these metrics on the scorecard provide answers to the following questions regarding financial performance:

☐ Are we profitable and getting a good return on our investment (ROI)?

☐ Are we managing our cash flow to ensure we can meet all of our obligations?

☐ Are we minimizing our financial risk?

☐ How does our future financial performance look?

☐ Are we growing in sales and market share?

For a government or nonprofit organization, this section of the scorecard typically answers the following questions:

☐ Do our outcomes provide good value for taxpayers and other stakeholders?

☐ Are we effectively managing spending against our budgets?

☐ Are we bringing in new sources of money and other resources?

☐ Are we continuing to lower our costs or at least improve the productivity of the resources we have?

Figure 8-1. Questions Answered by Strategic and Financial Metrics

Strategic Metrics

A *prerequisite* to coming up with a good set of strategic metrics is to have a clear and measurable vision, and well-defined strategies for achieving that vision. Metrics will be derived from either the vision itself, or the strategies used to achieve it. To illustrate this concept, we can revisit an organization mentioned in previous chapters: the Santa Clara Valley Water District in San Jose, California. The water district's vision is "Getting Greener, Getting Cleaner, and Getting Leaner," and the CEO's scorecard includes three analytics that provide data on the district's progress toward achieving that vision. The metrics shown in Figure 8-2 are derived from the three-part vision of the water district. Sub-metrics in each of the three analytics include both leading and lagging measures of how the district was doing at getting greener, cleaner, and leaner. The individual measures under each analytic are shown in yellow (clean), green (green), and blue (lean). In the figure, yellow is represented by light gray, green is represented by dark gray, and blue by black.

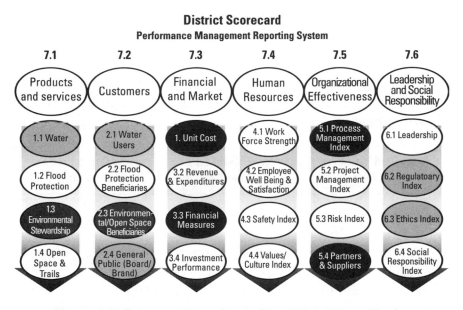

District Scorecard
Performance Management Reporting System

Figure 8-2. Scorecard from Santa Clara Valley Water District Showing Strategic metrics.

Two companies I worked with (Discover Card and Ericsson) had the same vision: Rank at least #3 in market share. Discover Card decided it would use three strategies to grow its market share:

1. First of all, the company needed to get more new card members or customers. This was to be accomplished through a marketing/advertising campaign that included direct mail, television, print, and radio ads. The company also came up with an attractive balance transfer option to get people to transfer their balances from Visa or MasterCard to Discover.
2. The second strategy involved signing up more merchants so that the Discover card was accepted at more establishments.
3. The third growth strategy was to develop new cards, which would attract a broader (and more diverse) segment of the population. For example, Discover created a premium "Black" card, appealing to higher-income and status-conscious customers. The company also offered more affinity cards, with links to customers' favorite universities, clubs, or other affiliations. New cards with artistic designs were also offered.

Discover created three strategic metrics for its scorecard, each linked to its strategies for growing market share. These metrics are shown in Figure 8-3.

New Card Members Analytic	New Merchants Analytic	New Cards/Product Analytic

Figure 8-3. Example of Strategic Metrics for the Discover Card Company

The metric for measuring new card members included lagging measures like the number of new card members, but it also included measures of the *quality* of those members and the *effectiveness* of direct mail and other marketing campaigns designed to bring in new customers.

Ericsson had a similar vision of growing market share and decided to focus on three strategies for doing so:

1. Increasing brand awareness and image among consumers,
2. Partnering with retailers, and
3. Increasing R&D and new product development.

Both companies also had market share as a metric in this section of their scorecards, because that was their ultimate vision. Market share is not an analytic; it is simply a measure of the market share percentage.

Norfolk Naval Shipyard repairs ships, aircraft carriers, and submarines for the U.S. Navy. It developed three strategic metrics for the Commanding Officer's dashboard. All three strategic measures are analytics or indices that are made up of multiple sub-metrics. The three strategic analytics are:

1. **Leadership Index:** provides data on the knowledge/skill gaps in the workforce;
2. **Alignment Index:** provides data on aligning goals, measures, strategies, and initiatives throughout the shipyard; and
3. **Customer Surprise Index:** provides management with data on how often and how badly the shipyard surprises its customers with cost overruns, missed deadlines, or quality problems.

Normally, these three metrics would go in other sections of the dashboard, but because they linked to the CO's vision, they were put in this segment of the dashboard. (Alternatively, the Leadership Index might go with other Human Resource metrics; the Alignment Index might go in the Organizational Effectiveness section; and the Customer Surprise Index might go in the Customer section of the Command Dashboard.)

Financial Metrics

This section of the scorecard rarely needs to be radically changed, because what is currently being measured will most likely continue to be measured. The big change will occur in the process of measurement and will involve combining a long list of individual measures into a few financial analytics. The toughest part of this will be selecting one index or analytic metric that provides leaders with an overall view of past performance. Some companies like EBITDA, some like profit, some like sales revenue, and some like stock price. The criteria listed in Figure 8-4 can help you decided which metrics best depict your financial health.

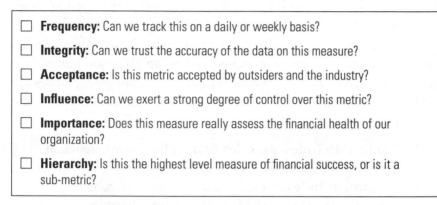

☐ **Frequency:** Can we track this on a daily or weekly basis?

☐ **Integrity:** Can we trust the accuracy of the data on this measure?

☐ **Acceptance:** Is this metric accepted by outsiders and the industry?

☐ **Influence:** Can we exert a strong degree of control over this metric?

☐ **Importance:** Does this measure really assess the financial health of our organization?

☐ **Hierarchy:** Is this the highest level measure of financial success, or is it a sub-metric?

Figure 8-4. Criteria to Consider When Choosing the Financial Metrics for Your Organization's Scorecard

Financial Analytics

If there is one area where executives tend to love lots of data, it is financial. In most companies, therefore, convincing senior leaders to come up with one analytic that best tells them about the financial health of their organization will be a tough sell. The trick is to show these leaders that "less is more" and that a Financial Analytic, which might be a combination of a series of individual, appropriately weighted metrics, is more efficient than a long list of individual traditional metrics. Figure 8-5 illustrates this concept.

Revenue Growth	Profit	Stock Price	ROI
20%	30%	30%	20%

Figure 8-5. Sample Weightings of Sub-Metrics for a Financial Analytic

The example in Figure 8-5 combines four lagging metrics of financial health into a single analytic. If the organization is hitting its targets on all four metrics, the analytic would show green and there would be no yellow or red warning light unless one unit of the company was not performing to standard. The best thing about an analytic like this is that two of the measures (revenue and stock price) have movement on a daily basis, and these two measures represent 50 percent of the analytic.

It is perfectly acceptable to combine individual metrics into an analytic even if the data for them is collected with different frequencies. If profit and ROI are calculated only once a month, but stock price and revenue change daily, the value of profit and ROI would stay the same for 30 days until the next month's statistics are entered.

The threshold for turning on the warning light can be as low as you want it to be. In some organizations, executives may only want to see a warning light if a business unit is not hitting its financial targets. In another company, they may want the warning light to come on if an individual product is not performing at the "green" level.

Past, Present, and Future Financial Measures

The ideal financial metrics on a balanced scorecard would include one metric that looks at the past, one that looks at the present, and one that looks at the future:

- Past measures are important outcomes that nothing can be done to improve today.
- Present metrics are those that can still be influenced to improve performance.
- Future metrics are measures that help predict an organization's future financial success.

Some examples are shown in Figure 8-6.

A simple example that translates Figure 8-6 into actual business practice comes from my consulting business. I track the following things (note that the analytic uses past, present, and future indicators):

- how much I billed the previous month (a past indicator),
- how much is in accounts receivable and when the invoice date was (a present indicator), and
- book sales (a future indicator).

Book sales are a future-focused financial metric that links to my consulting income, because if 100 people buy my book, 50 actually

Organization	Past	Present	Future
Navy Team One	Net Operating Revenue	Cost Performance Labor Days	Future Work
California State University, San Jose	Unit Costs vs. Benchmarks	Actual Spending vs. Budget	$ in New Products/Services
Lutheran Brotherhood (now Thrivent Financial)	Return on Equity	LB Value	Cost Savings
Aircraft Maintenance Company	Gross Margin	Project Spending vs. Budgets	Backlog & Contracts
Palomar Pomerado Hospitals	EBITDA	$/Patient Day	$ in New Funding

Figure 8-6. Examples of Past, Present, and Future Financial Metrics in Different Types of Organizations

read it, 2 of them typically call me, and 1 of them usually hires me to do some consulting or training work. Therefore, when I see a dip in book sales for a few months, I can predict that my consulting revenue will also dip in the next 3 to 6 months.

A future-focused financial metric for many manufacturing firms is orders. Future financial metrics are not forecasts; they are actual measures of performance. For the hospital listed in Figure 8-6, a future-focused metric is bringing in new money from grants and other sources.

The financial metrics you select might not be analytics or indices, but individual numbers. The two most common past-focused metrics on the scorecard of several businesses I have worked with are sales (in dollars) and gross margin (in percent):

1. Sales or revenue can be a tier-two metric under gross margin as shown in the example in Figure 8-7, or they can be a tier-one metric.

2. Gross margin dollars is a good metric because it provides a summary of the revenue and expenses in an organization and directly links to profitability, as long as you control overhead expenses.

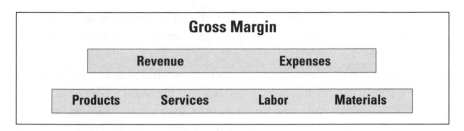

Figure 8-7. Example of Gross Margin Metric

Both sales/revenue and gross margin are preferable to measuring profit or ROI because they can be tracked on a daily basis: Although profit or ROI are the ultimate goals and outcomes of any business, they don't make the best scorecard metrics because they are generally only computed once a month, and most managers want to track dollars coming in and going out more frequently. Money comes in and goes out daily, so the gauges can be monitored often.

Future Financial Metrics

A concept that many people struggle with is that *future financial metrics are* not *forecasts applied to past metrics like sales or margins*. Future financial metrics are good or bad things that directly link to and help predict your performance on the outcome financial measures. There are many other metrics on your scorecard that may be predictive for your financial results. For example, a Customer Relationship Analytic is a measure that predicts future customer buying behavior and therefore, sales. Similarly, measuring employee productivity directly links to costs, which links to profits. In fact, most of the nonfinancial metrics should directly or indirectly link to the financial performance of a business—if they don't, you shouldn't be tracking them! What we are looking for in this section of the scorecard is a metric that is financial in nature and *directly* correlates to outcome financial metrics like sales or profits.

Companies such as Bose and Medtronic are both viewed as pioneers in their respective fields (audio and medical devices). A future-focused financial metric for these two firms might be sales from new products. Although this is a lagging metric (because the sales have already occurred), it also is a predictor of future revenue. The sales of a new product, such as noise-canceling headphones or an electronic device for minimizing pain, are likely to start out low. It takes awhile for people to become aware of a new product and want it. Once momentum builds, sales increase each year until the life cycle of the product starts to wind down and sales stabilize or decline. For companies like Bose and Medtronic, therefore, looking at first-year sales of a new product might be a great future-focused financial metric. The data from this metric can be extrapolated to predict, for example, that every 1 unit of a product sold the first year can translate to 10 units sold in the second year, 20 in the third year, and so forth.

The same logic applies when I look at book sales for my business. How many books I sold in the last six months is a lagging indicator, and I get a royalty check based on those book sales. However, my major source of income is not book royalties, it is consulting and training. So if my sole business was being an author, book royalty dollars would belong in the *lagging* or past section of my scorecard. But because I use books as a marketing strategy for my consulting business, book sales become a *leading* indicator of my consulting income.

Future financial metrics are often positive, but not always. In some companies, it is even more important to look at a negative metric. General Motors, which is teetering on the brink of bankruptcy, is a good example for illustrating this point. Although GM's market share has dwindled significantly from where it once was, it is still the largest car company in the world. The main cause of GM's woes is not slow car sales; the real problem is the company's obligations to retirees and existing workers. Thousands of dollars in costs for pensions and benefits go into the purchase price of each car GM sells. Union contracts that require GM to pay idle workers are also a major drain on what could be profits. A future-focused metric for a company like GM, therefore, might be financial obligations that the company knows it has to pay in the future.

Companies like United Airlines have had the same problem, and filing bankruptcy presented an opportunity to free themselves from many of these obligations, including union contracts and employee pensions. But while filing for bankruptcy may seem like a good short-term solution to making financial metrics look better, it often has a devastating impact on employee satisfaction, stock price, and customer confidence in your brand. This negative impact, moreover, can be a long-term headache.

Financial Metrics in Nonprofit and Government Organizations

Government and nonprofit organizations are not supposed to make money, but they certainly need to watch how they spend it, and they are accountable to taxpayers or others about whether or not they are getting good value for the money they spend. Like business organizations, these organizations can benefit from good financial analytics on their scorecards.

The Workforce Development Division (WDD) in the City of Los Angeles is one of the pioneers in city government in designing and implementing an analytics-based scorecard. The financial metrics on its scorecard are depicted in Figure 8-8, along with their relative weights and sub-metrics:

- Past financial metrics: The WDD can get comparative data from the U.S. Department of Labor on unit costs to provide services for youths, adults, and dislocated workers. Unit cost is a past-focused metric and is assigned a 10 percent weight in the overall Financial Analytic for WDD.
- Present-focused financial metrics. The WDD measures its actual spending versus its budget on a monthly basis. This is an important measure to watch to make sure that everyone stays within budget.
- Future-focused financial metrics. There are two future-focused financial metrics on the WDD scorecard:
  1. Financial Process Analytic: This is a measure of how the organization does at following rules and standards for financial management.
  2. $ in New Funds: This is not an analytic; instead, it is a measure of the total dollars the organization brings in from grants and other sources.

These four measures (1 past, 1 present, and 2 future) answer the following questions:

1. Are we making productive use of our resources to assist clients? (This is revealed by the Unit Cost measure.)
2. Are we adhering to our budgets? (This is revealed by the Budget Index.)
3. Are we following rules and procedures for managing the financial affairs of the division? (This question can be answered by the Process Analytic.)
4. Are we successful in bringing in funds from new sources? (This question is answered by measuring the $ in New Funds.)

LA Workforce Development Division			
Unit Cost Analytic	**Budget vs. Actual**	**Financial Process**	**$ in New Funds Analytic**
10%	20%	35%	35%
Audit Results Contractor Payments		Cycle Time	
80%		20%	
# of Findings		Severity of Findings	
50%		50%	

Figure 8-8. Example of the Financial Metrics for a Nonprofit Organization

Of the four metrics in the financial section of WDD's scorecard, only one is an analytic. The rest are single statistics that drill down by type of client served and service provided (unit cost), budget line items (budget versus actual), and source of additional resources ($ in new funds).

Chapter Summary

The strategic and financial section of your scorecard is the section where the metrics are the most unique to your organization. It is also the section that tends to have the fewest analytic metrics and more singular measures of statistics like sales and profits.

Collectively, the strategic metrics on this section of your scorecard should reveal how your organization is progressing toward achieving its vision. Strategic measures might address people issues, customer issues, financial factors, or other things. If you want to create a unique category on your scorecard for the strategic/vision metrics, it is perfectly fine to do so. The examples below illustrate how other organizations have customized their strategic metrics. One client's vision was to be listed among the "100 Best Companies to Work For" in *Fortune* Magazine. Because this company's entire vision was focused on its employees, it made sense that employee satisfaction and other related metrics, which would normally go in the people section of a scorecard, got put in the strategic section. Another client had a vision of being recognized as the best online banking site. Consequently, this organization's strategic measures included a Brand Analytic and customer measures that would typically be in other sections of the scorecard. If your vision is to double in sales in five years, then sales would probably be a metric to put in the strategic section of the scorecard.

In a business, growth and profitability are usually important measures. In contrast, in a nonprofit organization, financial measures tend to look more at value received for the dollars expended. The financial section of the scorecard tends to look similar in most businesses, but government and nonprofit organizations sometimes find it difficult to come up with meaningful financial metrics that drive the right behavior in employees.

The challenge for all types of organizations with financial measures is coming up with metrics that are *leading indicators*. All traditional financial metrics are measures of the past or lagging. A good balanced scorecard should include one or two financial measures that are predictive or leading. Gross margin is a *lagging* indicator. A leading financial measure is something real that you can count and correlates to future financial success. Future metrics might include proposals or bids submitted, orders, contracts, or agreements with customers.

The ideal Strategic and Financial section of your scorecard should have 2 or 3 strategic metrics linked to the vision and 3 or 4 financial metrics, with at least one of these being future-focused or leading.

Chapters 4 through 8 of this book provide examples and guidance on how to construct a balanced scorecard based on a series of analytic gauges. Having the best scorecard with the right metrics, however, will not do anything to improve your organization's performance unless managers know how to improve the aspects of performance being measured. Chapter 9 discusses how to move the needles on your gauges—specifically, how to go from performance *measurement* to performance *management*.

Key Points to Keep in Mind
About Strategic and Financial Metrics and Analytics

☐ It is important to separate metrics that focus on your *vision* from those that address the *mission* of your organization.

☐ Strategic metrics provide management with data on how well their top strategies are working to get to their vision.

☐ Strategic measures will change as the vision and strategy change.

☐ All organizations need to have financial measures on their scorecards.

☐ Financial measures tend to vary greatly depending on industry/field and the preference of the organization's leaders.

☐ Traditional financial measures all tend to be lagging indicators, and there are often too many of them.

☐ Financial metrics may not be true analytics, but overall numbers like profit or gross margin that can be drilled down to many individual measures of cost and revenue.

☐ Predictive financial metrics that help tell leaders how the organization will be performing in the future need to be included on the scorecard.

☐ Predictive or leading financial metrics are not forecasts but real things that can be measured—such as orders, contracts, or proposals.

9

Beyond the Balanced Scorecard: From Performance Measurement to Performance Management

Performance measures by themselves will not do anything to improve performance. Simply measuring some aspect of performance is not the same as *improving* it. The goal of a scorecard in an organization is to provide decision makers with data they need to identify and solve problems and to improve performance where necessary. The challenge facing most designers of scorecards is coming up with meaningful measures that have integrity. Most measures that are easy to track are of dubious value and are sometimes worse than not having any data at all. Another problem is that measurement can be time consuming and expensive: The more we try to make the measures better, and the more often we collect and report data, the more money we spend.

Many organizations have come to recognize the challenges associated with past and even with some current measurement models and are seeking new ways to define and use accurate metrics to improve performance. The purpose of this chapter is to outline how performance measurement in organizations is likely to change over the next 10 years or so. Because these changes are rooted in the past, it begins with a brief look at the history of performance measurement.

Scorecards Over the Last 30 Years

If you look back to the 1980s, most government organizations did not measure their performance at all. With the exception of periodic studies or activity measures (such as how many reports were generated or clients were served), there were no real ongoing performance measures. Businesses, on the other hand, have always measured financial and some operational aspects of performance. As business organizations grew and changed, the number of metrics in these organizations proliferated. This trend continued until about the mid-1990s, when the prevailing wisdom changed and business leaders began to realize that fewer metrics were better. Executives began to look for a few key statistics that would tell them how their organizations were performing and slowly moved away from wading through volumes of data and endless spreadsheets.

By about 2005, many executives were becoming disillusioned with the search for 'magic' metrics that would really tell them about organizational performance without complicated statistics and drill downs. Even more recently, many executives have become disillusioned with strategy maps, which often fail to produce process metrics that can be linked to important outcomes. What these executives have discovered is that most strategy maps are not based on research and data collection, but on prevailing opinions, logic, and wishful thinking. While process measures are showing green, outcomes remain in the red zone. The underlying problem boils down to one significant truth: *Strategy maps are often a systematic documentation of a long string of assumptions and hypotheses that are rarely tested.* Because the diagrams look so convincing, no one thinks to question their validity.

Obviously, most business and nonprofit organizations have changed over the last 30 years. In the process, they have also changed the way they measure performance. Figure 9-1 summarizes these changes.

Flabby Middle-Aged Scorecards

Suzanne Stroh of the University of California Office of the President has observed that some scorecards are approaching middle age. A corollary to this is that performance measurement systems in some organizations are not necessarily getting better with age. Stroh's contention is that some measurement systems are slipping into flabby

Stage I Scorecards Prior to 1980

- Financial and operational metrics
- Productivity metrics
- More measures are better
- All lagging metrics

Stage II Scorecards 1980–1995

- Financial and operational metrics
- Customer satisfaction metrics
- Quality metrics
- Process metrics
- Even more measures than Stage I

Stage III Scorecards 1996–2005

- Balanced scorecard adopted
- Fewer metrics are better
- Customer metrics
- Financial metrics
- Internal metrics
- Innovation, learning, and growth metrics
- All measures are singular metrics
- Strategy maps used to develop metrics linked to goals and outcomes

Figure 9-1. 30 Years of Evolution of Performance Measurement

middle age and declining toward "moribund." She defines the characteristics of a flabby middle-aged scorecard as follows:

- Inconsistent management support or loss of interest in nonfinancial metrics
- Serious disagreements among leaders about what to measure, when to measure, and how to measure
- Distrust in the integrity of the data
- Rigid compliance to a textbook scorecard architecture
- "Flavor-of-the-month" metrics linked to management initiatives or pet strategies
- Targets that appear too hard or too easy

- Static measures year after year
- Evidence of game playing to make performance look good on important metrics
- Lack of use of scorecard software or reporting tools

Like Suzanne Stroh, I have observed a lot of flabby middle-aged scorecards in corporations and government organizations. A few need major surgery to survive. Flawed metrics need to be removed, and old worn gauges need to be replaced with improved gauges that better assess performance. Coming up with the scorecard was hard enough; many organizations just want to be done with it so they can move on to more interesting initiatives. But the scorecard should not be abandoned. Instead, it needs to evolve, continuously improve, and mature, as do all systems in organizations. By the same token, an organization that has been working on implementing a good performance management system need not slip into flabby middle age. With continued evaluation and improvement, both the organization and the scorecard can mature gracefully and become better each successive year.

Stage IV Scorecards: Lean and Aligned

At Stage III (where all the five companies in the APQC study would fall), scorecards are well balanced and contain 12 to 16 metrics, but each metric is a singular statistic that is being used to evaluate a complex dimension of organizational performance. Process or leading indicators are derived from strategy maps or brainstorming sessions, but there is no real evidence backing up the links between various measures and outcomes.

Organizations with Stage IV Scorecards have the characteristics listed in Figure 9-2. You can use this as a checklist guide when developing your own scorecard. As you can see, a Stage IV Scorecard is a very sophisticated set of numbers or charts that are used to assess the ongoing performance of the organization.

Red Is Not Dead

A challenge that many organizations face as they implement a performance management system is that people fear seeing a red gauge in

☐ Most metrics are analytics comprised of several tiers of sub-metrics.

☐ Metrics are evenly balanced across past, present, and future time perspectives.

☐ Metrics have evolved and changed as the organization learned better ways of measuring performance.

☐ Old metrics have been dropped from the scorecard when they are no longer useful and replaced with new and better ones.

☐ Most managers and employees look at the scorecard at least weekly, and most review performance daily.

☐ Scorecard software is used to display real-time data on individual desktops and in meetings.

☐ Meetings to review performance are shorter than they used to be, and most meeting time is spent discussing gauges that show performance that is below targets.

☐ Senior leaders spend as much time reviewing and discussing nonfinancial performance as they do financial metrics.

☐ All employees at all levels have their own scorecards for their jobs, and the different levels of scorecards are well aligned.

☐ Leading or process metrics have been correlated to outcome measures using research and experimentation.

☐ Red, yellow, and green targets or ranges have been set based on thorough research.

☐ Targets are adjusted as needed when additional data is gathered.

☐ Links have been established between measures of employee satisfaction, customer satisfaction, and outcome measures such as growth and profits.

☐ Strategic metrics have been added to scorecards to provide data on progress being made to achieve an organization's vision.

☐ Checks and balances are in place to ensure data integrity.

☐ Performance data is used as an analytical tool to diagnose the causes of problems rather than to find someone to blame for a "red gauge."

☐ Managers have learned to ask four questions about each performance metric:
  1. How are we doing right now against our targets?   (LEVEL)
  2. How have we performed over the last few months/years?   (TREND)
  3. What is causing us to perform this way?   (ANALYSIS)
  4. What are we doing to improve or maintain performance?   (ACTIONS)

Figure 9-2. Characteristics of the Stage IV Scorecard

their area. Red means you screwed up or did something wrong, and if you own a red gauge, you will be the focus of senior management in the dreaded monthly meeting. No one wants a red gauge, so finding one often leads to cover-ups and manipulation of the data to ensure that performance looks green. In the real estate business, for example, an agent may hand out customer surveys on transactions only to clients who are happy with a transaction or the agent's performance. This selective surveying ensures that reports on customer/client satisfaction always show green levels of performance.

Another thing that commonly occurs when people fear red gauges is that people will learn to set targets that can easily achieve "green" levels of performance. This is human nature, but the practice is much more prevalent in companies where fear of showing poor performance is enabled by a culture of punishment. If a company has made a habit of beating people up over poor performance, the scorecard will soon begin to reflect this response. When performance measured on scorecards is poor, performance review meetings are also poor. Most of the meeting time is spent defending, arguing, and challenging the validity of the data. A military organization, which spent about $100,000 to get a professional employee satisfaction survey done, recently experienced this problem. To begin with, only about 16 percent of the 8,000 employees filled out the survey (the most important statistic). Of those who did, the majority responded that they were not satisfied or "engaged" in their jobs. Rather than trying to find out why morale was so low and what could be done about it, the organization blasted the guy who suggested spending the money on the outside survey, pointing out that the data did not reflect reality (turnover was almost nonexistent) and condemning the idea of measuring morale using a survey in the first place. In other words, the meeting became a destructive blame and defend cycle rather than a constructive problem-solving session.

Other organizations have a better approach to red zones on scorecards. Bob Palladino, formerly of Crown Castle (manufacturer of cell phone antennas), found that the company had to come up with a slogan, *"Red is not dead,"* to keep reminding people what performance measurement is really all about. Once the company culture began to emphasize that a red gauge does not necessarily mean that someone screwed up or did not do his or her job, measurement (and performance) improved. It is not surprising, therefore, that Crown Castle was one of the five companies selected by APQC in 2004 as having one of the best scorecards in America. Crown Castle's Palladino explained that one benefit of the phrase "Red is not dead"was that the nature of the company's review meetings changed dramatically. Instead of being a venue for jumping all over someone with a red gauge, the meetings became an opportunity to focus on *diagnosing* and *solving* performance problems.This is precisely where you need to be to in the Phase IV level of maturity with your scorecard.

It is always important to keep in mind that a red level of performance or downward trend might be caused by a wide variety of factors outside of the organization. It is equally important for people who measure performance to understand what causes red levels and recommend appropriate change(s). This is why the Analysis section of the scorecard is so important. In the Analysis section, the metric owner needs to explain *why* performance is below target or declining. That explanation should be supplemented with evidence or data whenever possible. The person who owns the metric is also responsible for completing the Action Plan field that explains what is going to be done about the low level of performance. Even if the cause is something outside of the organization's control, something can usually be done to improve performance or reverse a declining trend.

So, a red gauge does not mean someone is dead. It only means you need to discover why something is red and devise a plan for dealing with it.You are only dead if you don't know why and don't have an appropriate action plan!

> *Red is only dead if you don't know why*
> *and are not doing anything about it.*

Limitations of a Balanced Scorecard

Organizations that think having a great balanced scorecard is all they need to drive them to excellence are sadly misled. A scorecard simply provides *data*. Looking at a scorecard of your department's performance is no different from getting on a scale and looking at your weight: Both provide you with data. Just looking at the scale will not make you thinner, and just looking at your organization's performance will not improve it. Taking action or changing your current approach is what is needed to drive improvement. In the wise words of consultant Aubrey Daniels and his son James, coauthors of *Performance Management—Changing Behavior That Drives Organizational Effectiveness* (2004): *"A great many people in business think that measuring a problem is tantamount to solving it. If measurement alone changed behavior, there would be no fat people, no one would smoke, and everyone would exercise because all of these behaviors and their results can be easily measured."*

Seeing that you have gained 5 pounds may or may not drive a change in behavior. Seeing that you have gained 20 might make it more likely that you will do something about it. In other words, the redder the performance gauge, the more likely that you take some sort of action. This is not always the case, however. You might weigh yourself every week, consistently see that you are 75 pounds overweight, and decide that you are just cursed with bad genetics and do nothing about it.

Reviewing performance data can result in the same sort of action or inaction. Often the reaction to a red gauge is to deny the validity of the data, or to blame it on factors outside of your control, just as our big guy does by blaming bad genes for his weight problem. At other times, the reaction to a red gauge is to take some action to make it green. The key to making sure the action is the correct one is to do an analysis before deciding on a course of action. For example, our heavy friend might not want to embark on a diet or exercise program without first consulting a doctor. The doctor might find out he has a thyroid problem, prescribe some medication, and put together a diet and exercise regime that actually works. A recent client had its employee satisfaction gauge (measured via annual survey) turn red. Teams were formed and various initiatives were developed to improve morale, including a recognition and reward program, employee newsletter, and more team building events. The following year morale had not improved. After holding focus groups with employees, the client learned that they did not care about the reward and recognition program, the newsletter, or team-building events. What they wanted was two things: 1) more frequent and thorough communication from management on what was going on in the company and 2) a "thank you" from their bosses when they put in extra effort or accomplish something important. The lesson here is that it is important to analyze the causes of a red gauge before jumping to actions that may not solve the problem.

Linking Scorecards and Knowledge Management

One thing that some companies are doing to make the scorecard a more useful tool for improving performance is to put links on the scorecard to their knowledge management databases. Performance-soft, the leading provider of scorecard software, is currently working on some new software that will link the two systems together. At present, a scorecard identifies areas of poor performance and allows you to drill down to find the exact location and source of a problem. It does not determine its root cause or course of action for improving performance. This is where the links to the knowledge database comes in. Click on a link connected to a particular analytic, and you will be given a menu of choices for information on the likely cause for the performance problem and possible solutions. The example below illustrates how this works in practice.

Let's say you are a plant manager, and you have noticed a sharp decline in employee satisfaction. You drill down into the data and find out that the problem is worst in your engineering department. The knowledge management (KM) database provides you with information on typical causes of dissatisfaction for engineers and technical professionals. The KM database might include a series of diagnostic questions to allow you to further diagnose the root cause, and will then branch you to a summary of possible actions to improve morale among the engineers.

This linking of KM and the scorecard makes the system a much more useful tool for managing and improving performance rather than just looking at it. Connecting your scorecard to your KM database is hardly enough to ensure excellent performance, however. It is a move in the right direction, but it is just one of many things that must be put into place to drive performance.

Performance Management vs. Performance Appraisal

A scorecard is nothing more than a mechanism for providing people with feedback on their performance. As suggested in Chapter 5 of this book, the scorecard might also provide information on external factors that impact performance. Regardless of how comprehensive your scorecard is, however, it is just information. Even linking it to KM databases is just a way of giving the viewer more information. Do a Google search on the phrase "performance management," and you will find a lot of links to companies that offer performance appraisal and succession planning systems. This alone should tell you that a performance management system is much more than a mechanism for providing employees with feedback: It is above all a mechanism that requires follow-up action.

> Performance *management* and performance *appraisal* are two completely different things!

Most performance appraisal systems provide feedback on performance, and some do this quite well. The problem is that very few of these systems are designed to guide and improve performance, something that the scorecard does exceptionally well. One of the underlying reasons for this is frequency of data gathering. Another is data integrity. Many appraisal systems gather performance measurement data once or twice a year. To make matters worse, the data gathered is often based on a totally subjective assessment of performance. A scorecard, on the other hand, provides *daily, weekly, and monthly feedback on quantitative and qualitative measures of performance*. In fact, some organizations have found that the scorecard replaces the need for a separate appraisal system. They may create individual development plans based on scorecard results, but there is no need for a separate evaluation of how an employee has performed during a given year.

Even a scorecard, however, is simply an aggregation of all performance data. In order to turn this information into performance, you need a good performance management system, which consists of a number of environmental components and human resource systems.

Components of a Performance Management System

The various components of a performance management system are depicted in Figure 9-3. (For additional information on this model, consult the excellent book *Human Competence—Engineering Worthy Performance* by Thomas F. Gilbert.) Note that the two main resources of the system are people and environment.

Environmental Factors

Information	*Resources*	*Consequences*
Job descriptions	Budget $	Promotions
Standards/Rules	People	More authority
Procedures	Tools/Equipment	More autonomy
Goals/expectations	Information Technology	Bonus
Feedback/Scorecard	Facilities	Raise
References/Knowledge	Suppliers	Recognition
Training	Workload	Dismissal/Discipline

People Factors

Capacity	*Knowledge & Skills*	*Motives & Values*
Intelligence	Technical/Job	Personal Goals
Physical capabilities	Communication	Values/Ethics
Prerequisite abilities	Analytical	Motives
Stress Tolerance	Tools/Equipment	Passion/Fun
Health	Managerial	Life Stage
Maturity	Experience	Rewards/Punishment

Figure 9-3. Performance Management Components

Environmental Factors

Most performance problems are not caused by people; they are caused by the environment. In fact, about 70 to 80 percent of performance problems are environmental. For this reason, all of the environmental factors listed in Figure 9-3 need to be in place for performance to excel. A lack of clarity about expectations or responsibilities can cause a problem, just as a lack of timely feedback or feedback based on flawed metrics (scorecard) can. Many organizations get dramatic improvements in performance just by developing scorecards for all levels of employees so that everyone gets daily and weekly feedback on how they are performing their jobs. If the scorecards are designed properly, regular feedback like this also tends to improve employee satisfaction. People like getting regular feedback on how they are performing. What they don't like is a once-a-year subjective evaluation of how they did all year.

Having a good set of instructions or guidelines can also be useful for a new task or one that is performed infrequently.

Performance problems are also caused by a lack of proper resources. If you give some mediocre people some great tools and equipment, they will often do a great job. Many government organizations, for example, are constrained by outdated information technology and ever-shrinking budgets. With the proper resources, they could be achieving much higher levels of performance.

Consequences are one of the most important and most often forgotten factors in a performance management system. If you want good performance from people, you must have "positive consequences" for good performance, and these must be personal, immediate, powerful, and certain. If you hit your sales goal, the team responsible gets an all-expenses-paid trip to Maui for five days. The message this sends shows that you have noticed good performance, that you give credit where credit is due, and that you are willing to acknowledge good performance with something better than lip service. Incentives of this kind can and do motivate most people.

Unfortunately, the real consequences operating in many organizations drive the opposite of good performance. Star performers simply get more work or more challenging assignments, while mediocre performers get to slack off and get the same pay as the star performers.

Suggesting there might be a profit-sharing bonus of $1,000 at the end of the year will not drive much performance either. The consequence is not powerful enough, not certain, delayed, and usually not directly tied to an individual's job performance. Moreover, good consequences need not be money or tangible things. In fact, often a powerful consequence is a "Thank you" from the boss for a job well done (if this is personal, immediate, and certain—i.e., it should be part of the organization's culture).

Negative consequences, such as the possibility of getting fired, do not do much to motivate many poor performers because legal and other constraints make it very difficult to fire people in most organizations.

A performance problem can be caused by any one of the variables outlined in the Environmental Factors section of Figure 9-3. Implementing a balanced scorecard and knowledge management system will not get you good performance if you do not supply appropriate tools and other resources to get the job done. Drawing process models and writing procedures will not improve performance unless there are positive consequences for following them. A performance management system is, after all, a system, and systems have inputs, processes, and outputs. All of these factors need to be in place and properly aligned if you expect to achieve outcomes like growth, profits, and loyal customers.

People Factors

The people in most work settings today are a vital factor in achieving good performance. All military and government organizations, healthcare and educational institutions, and most businesses are heavily dependent on their employees to achieve good performance. Author Jim Collins suggests that getting the "right people on the bus" is one of the most important ingredients in creating a high-performing company. Of course, if you hire great people and put them in a dysfunctional environment, they will not perform well, so you should never underestimate the importance of engineering the work environment properly to drive performance. In fact, one thing exceptional managers know is that *it is much easier to hire good people than it is to engineer the work setting for exceptional performance.*

All people involved in doing a job or task need the right capacity, motives and values, and knowledge and skills.

Capacity. Capacity refers to intelligence, strength, endurance/stress tolerance, health, and prerequisite abilities, such as empathy, communication, and other factors that tend to be inherited. Capacity factors are things that people either are born with or acquire at an early age. These are factors that employers look for when hiring. Selecting a person who does not have the required capacities for a job pretty much guarantees failure and poor performance. My dad, for example, wanted to be a pilot while in the Air Force. He was able to pass all the tests except one: the vision test. No amount of training or feedback would have allowed my dad to become an excellent pilot because he lacked the required capacity to perform this job well.

Motives and Values. Like capacity, motives and values are something to look for rather than teach. No two people are the same; what motivates us is unique rather than generic. Punishment for one person may be a reward to another. Personal goals and aspirations are also unique and pretty much impossible to change, so employers try to line up a job or career with employees' own goals. Some people are turned on by a challenge, others prefer an easy job; some are motivated by money, others are not; some are turned on by power, others are not. The bottom line is that we are all different in what we want from a job, and this makes matching the right person to the right job a challenge for many organizations.

Finding a way to earn a living and do something you have passion for is tough for most of us. We often fall into doing something that pays the bills. Most musicians and artists have passion for their work, but a great artist or musician will probably never be able to afford a new car, let alone a house, whereas a mediocre businessman or government employee can usually have a house and a fairly new car and even take a couple of vacations each year. Consequently, many of us forget about doing something we have passion for, and instead, go for some mind-numbing job that offers security and a good paycheck. Placing an employee in a job he or she has passion for is a tremendous driver for achieving high performance: All people put more effort into a job they enjoy doing.

Knowledge and Skills. Hiring smart people with the right values and motives is not enough—they need to have the knowledge and skills to do the job. All employees tend to have the basic knowledge and skills required to do their jobs, but differences in the level of that knowledge and those skills can be huge. Thousands of people, for example, have the knowledge and skills to be decent golfers, but very few (if any) can play like Tiger Woods.

Finding employees with levels of knowledge and skill that are superior to most is a major factor in achieving exceptional performance levels. Sometimes, as many high-tech companies are seeing today, the search for these people is difficult. It used to be that the best people wanted to work for Microsoft and HP and other well-known firms. Today, the talent wars between these industry giants have been exacerbated by Google and other, even newer companies. Many people from established companies are leaving to work for these new companies, often because they are not as slow and bureaucratic as some of the older firms have become.

Some organizations have responded to shortages of skilled and knowledgeable workers by attempting to fill the gap in people skills and human experience with some knowledge management database. This is something of a scam because no database is ever going to take the place of a superstar performer who has had years of experience honing his or her skills. Access to the right knowledge can help incompetent employees muddle their way through assignments, but they will probably never be as good as a top-notch professional. (I can study my *Time-Life Home Improvement* books and probably replace an old faucet, or install some drywall, but I will never be able to do it as well or as quickly as a professional who has been doing it for 20 years.)

Action Plan for Improving
Your Performance Management System

Most of this book discusses tools and strategies that improve the way you measure performance in your organization. More comprehensive metrics gathered more frequently should help identify and solve problems more quickly—and help you improve performance where it is low or declining. However, you can never forget that having a great scorecard is only one component in a performance management system. Here are some other related actions you should consider:

☐ Clearly define responsibilities and expectations for all employees.

☐ Document processes and make the documentation easily accessible to all.

☐ Define specific targets for all metrics and base the targets on hard data—not guesswork.

☐ Design scorecards for all levels of employees, from the boss down to individual workers.

☐ Buy scorecard software that can be used with analytic metrics, and allow all employees to access the software at their desks or work areas.

☐ Use the scorecard as your performance appraisal process, and do developmental planning once a year.

☐ Ensure that goals, measures, strategies, and initiatives are all aligned.

☐ Research links between process and output/outcome measures—don't rely on strategy maps or logic.

☐ Learn about the interrelationships between the metrics on your scorecard.

☐ Continuously refine and improve your performance measures, targets, and strategies.

☐ Document best practices and important knowledge in knowledge management databases, and provide access to employees and partners.

☐ Provide interactive skill-building training to teach important knowledge and skills to employees.

☐ Buy the best tools and equipment you can afford.

☐ Ensure that teams are provided with adequate budgets and other resources needed to perform well on the job.

☐ Make sure your information technology is the best you can afford and meets the needs of users.

- [ ] Link bonuses and raises to scorecards.

- [ ] Develop creative ways to reinforce and recognize good performance.

- [ ] Hire the smartest and most experienced people you can afford.

- [ ] Invest in continuously training your people so they can hone their knowledge and skills.

- [ ] Screen potential new hires for their motives and values rather than trying to change them.

- [ ] Place people in jobs they have passion for and in which they are most likely to be successful.

Final Thoughts

Developing a meaningful scorecard that really tells an organization how it is performing is incredibly difficult. One of the most important conclusions of the APQC scorecard benchmarking study is that even the best companies in the world are struggling with implementation of a scorecard that tells them about the overall health of their enterprises.

The current trend toward more simplistic singular metrics is exactly the direction that is needed. But even here, it is necessary to exercise caution. Reducing a complex performance dimension, such as customer relationships, to a single question on a survey is a very stupid and dangerous practice. The best scorecards are neither too complex nor too simplistic. They include meaningful and comprehensive metrics that tell organizations how they are really performing. A number of leading organizations today are introducing analytics into their balanced scorecards. By reviewing analytics rather than singular metrics, managers and leaders are given a better overall view of major aspects of performance. Analytics provide better data than any single metric on its own, and they provide for easy analysis and drill-down into details, using scorecard software. Only through the use of current scorecard software is it possible to have a scorecard that comprises analytic metrics and is still easy to use and understand by all levels of employees. Begin the process of refining your scorecard by introducing a few analytics to replace singular measures. Then refine and improve the metrics each year until most of your executive-level gauges are analytics.

As organizations and their leaders become more sophisticated, so too must the measures they use to assess performance. Running an organization will never become a science like engineering, but we will see a more scientific approach applied to measuring and managing business performance. Ten years from now, we will marvel at how businesses assessed performance and made important decisions based on such crude metrics as we see on many of today's balanced scorecards.

Appendix

The samples that follow depict analytic-based scorecards from a variety of types of organizations. Included are examples from healthcare, water, city government, corporate, finance function, and an educational institution. In each case, the examples include the overall scorecard and one drill-down screen for a particular section of the scorecard. These examples are not from any specific companies or organizations, but are an amalgamation of a variety of organization's scorecards. The examples are presented using PB Views software from Performancesoft, the market leader in balanced scorecard software.

Healthcare Overall Performance View

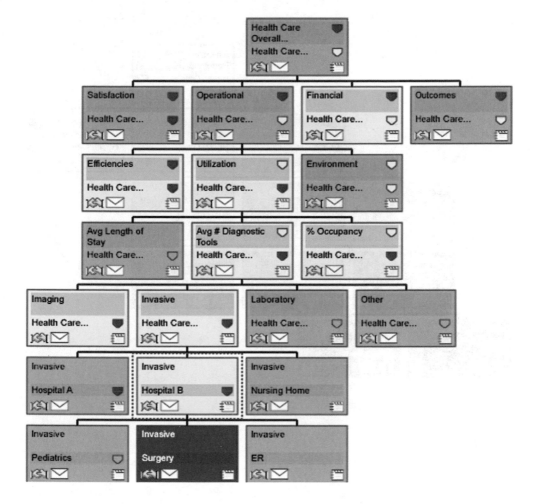

Healthcare Financial Performance View

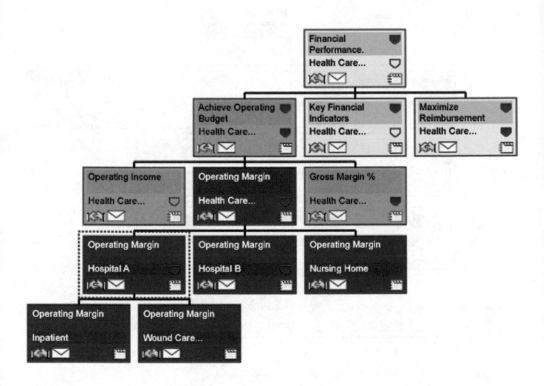

JCAHO Performance View

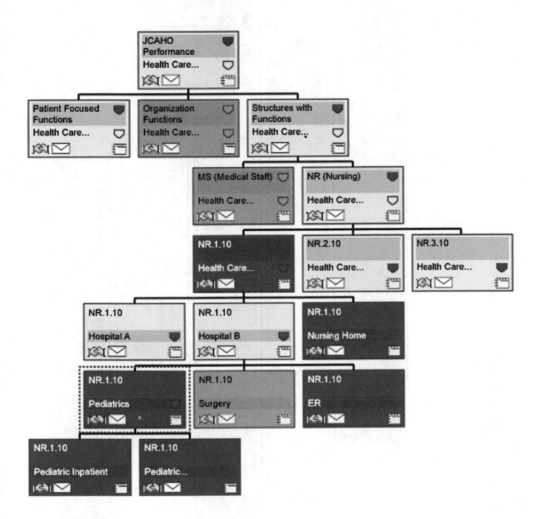

Utility Water/Wastewater Overall Performance View

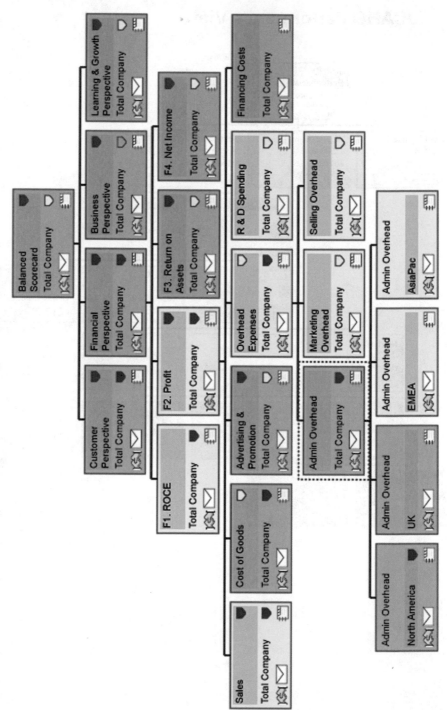

Utility Water/Wastewater IT Performance View

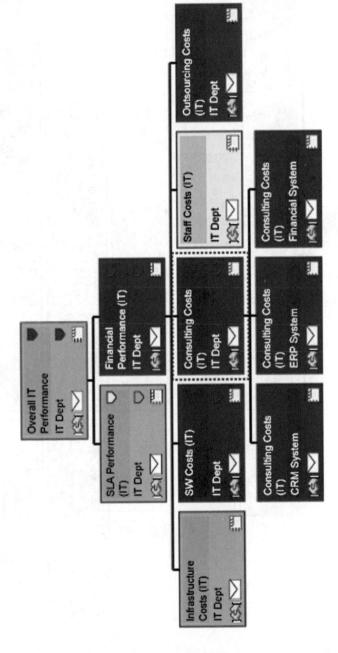

City Government Overall Performance View

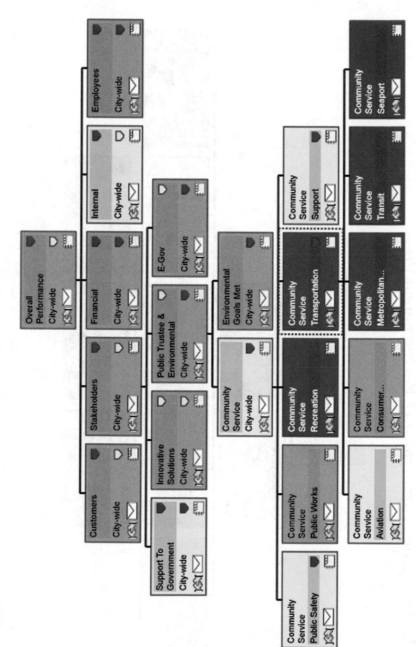

City Government Financial Performance View

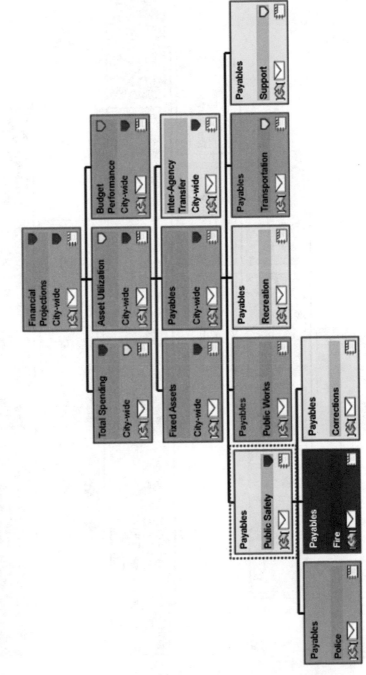

Corporate Overall Performance View

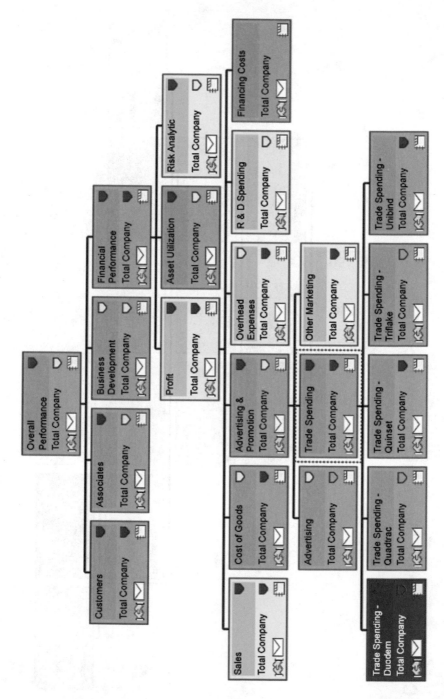

Corporate Balanced Scorecard View

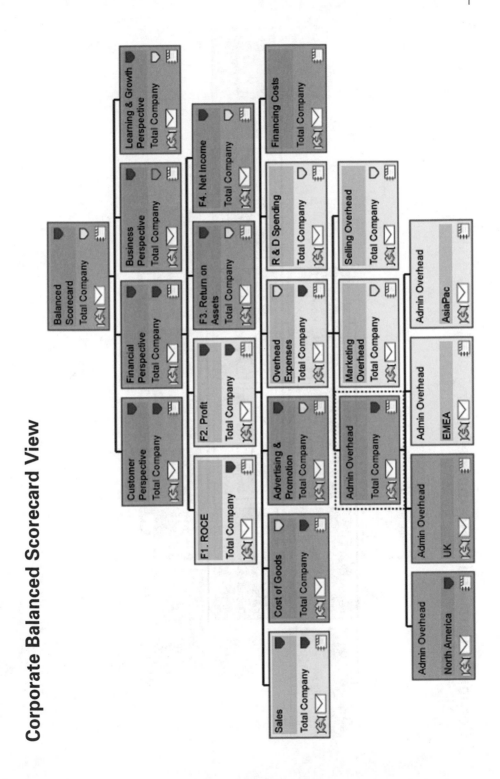

Corporate Financial Performance View

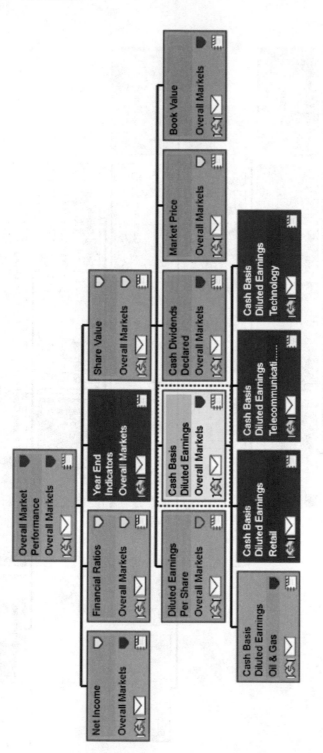

Banking Overall Performance View

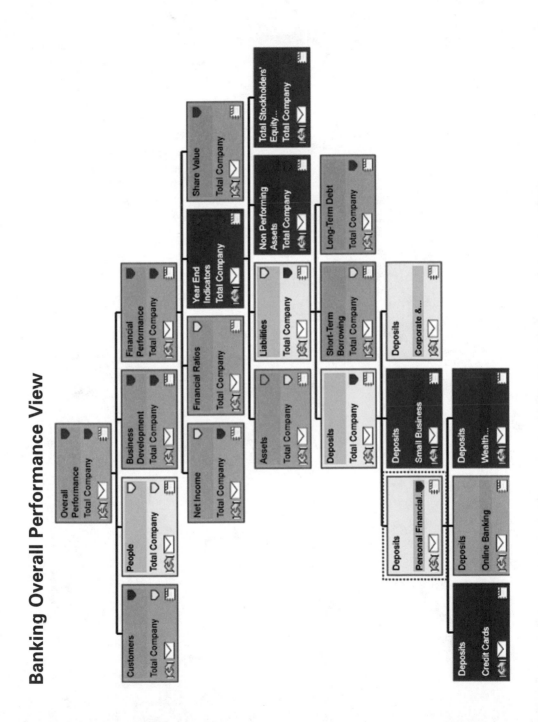

References

Brown, Mark Graham. *Keeping Score—Using the Right Metrics to Drive World-Class Performance*. New York: AMACOM/Productivity Press, 1996.

———. *Winning Score—How to Design and Implement Organizational Scorecards*. New York: Productivity Press, 2000.

Brown, Mark G., and Raynold A. Svenson. "Measuring R&D Productivity." *Research and Technology Management*, November/December 1998. (RTM Classic, originally published 1988).

Buckingham, Marcus, and Curt Coffman. *First Break All the Rules—What the World's Greatest Managers do Differently*. New York: Simon & Schuster, 1999.

Daniels, Aubrey C., and James E. Daniels. *Performance Management—Changing Behavior That Drives Organizational Effectiveness*. Atlanta: Performance Management Publications, 2004.

Fisher, Donald C. *Homeland Security Assessment Manual— A Comprehensive Organizational Assessment Based on the Baldrige Criteria*. Milwaukee: ASQ Press, 2004.

Gilbert, Thomas F. *Human Competence—Engineering Worthy Performance*. Silver Spring, MD: International Society for Performance and Instruction, 1996.

Gitomer, Jeffrey. *Customer Satisfaction Is Worthless, Customer Loyalty Is Priceless: How to Make Customers Love You, Keep Them Coming Back, and Tell Everyone They Know*. Bard Press, 1998.

Hamm, Steve. "Speed Demons: How smart companies are creating new products and whole new businesses almost overnight." *Business Week*, March 27, 2006: 68–76.

Higgins, Lisa, and Becki Hack. *Measurement in the 21st Century White Paper*. American Productivity and Quality Center, 2004.

Hubbard, Edward E. *The Diversity Scorecard*. Boston: Butterworth-Heinmann, 2003.

Joni, Saj-nicole A. "The Geography of Trust." *Harvard Business Review*, March, 2004: 82–88.

Kaplan, Robert S., and David P. Norton. *Alignment—Using the Balanced Scorecard to Create Synergy*. Cambridge, MA: Harvard Business School Press, 2006.

Malony, David, and Robert Bustos-McNeil. "A New Window into CRM." *Strategy + Business*, Spring, 2004: 28–31.

Morris, Betsy. "The 100 Best Companies to Work for 2006—The Best Place to Work Now." *Fortune*, January 23, 2006: 79–108.

Orey, Michael. "Forecast: Is that a lawsuit blowing in?" *Business Week*, April 10, 2006: 14.

Phillips, Jack, and Patricia Pullman Phillips (Eds.). *Measuring Intellectual Capital (in action)*. ASTD, 2002.

Reichfield, Frederick. *Loyalty Rules! How Today's Leaders Build Lasting Relationships*. Cambridge, MA: Harvard Business School Press, 2003.

Rigley, Jennifer. "Overcoming CRM Failure in Financial Services: What's Not Working." crmguru.com. February 18, 2003.

Stroh, Suzanne. *Performance-Based Management System Maturity Review Proposal*. Unpublished paper, 2000.

Surmacz, Jon. "A Second Look at CRM." *cio.com/metrics*. June 11, 2003.

Index